TELEVISION AND PRESIDENTIAL POLITICS

THE BROOKINGS INSTITUTION

The Brookings Institution is an independent organization engaged in research and education in the social sciences. Its principal purposes are to aid in the development of sound public policies and to provide advanced training for students in the social sciences.

The Institution was founded December 8, 1927 as a consolidation of three antecedent organizations: the Institute for Government Research, 1916; the Institute of Economics, 1922; and the Robert Brookings Graduate School of Economics and Government, 1924.

The general administration of the Institution is the responsibility of a self-perpetuating Board of Trustees. In addition to this general responsibility the By-Laws provide that, "It is the function of the Trustees to make possible the conduct of scientific research and publication, under the most favorable conditions, and to safeguard the independence of the research staff in the pursuit of their studies and in the publication of the results of such studies. It is not a part of their function to determine, control, or influence the conduct of particular investigations or the conclusions reached." The immediate direction of the policies, program, and staff of the Institution is vested in the President, who is assisted by an advisory council, chosen from the professional staff of the Institution.

In publishing a study, the Institution presents it as a competent treatment of a subject worthy of public consideration. The interpretations and conclusions in such publications are those of the author or authors and do not necessarily reflect the views of other members of the Brookings staff or of the administrative officers of the Institution.

Television and Presidential Politics

THE EXPERIENCE IN 1952 AND THE PROBLEMS AHEAD

CHARLES A. H. THOMSON

THE BROOKINGS INSTITUTION

Washington, D.C.

1956

Preface

MUCH has been written about television, but relatively little consideration has been given to the relationship of television to the political process and still less to the issues of public policy that are presented by this use of the medium. This small book is a pioneering effort to examine these subjects, to see what television has meant to date in presidential politics, to consider what its future may be, and to encourage a further examination of the problems it presents.

The present study was initially undertaken by Charles A. H. Thomson as a part of a larger investigation of the presidential nominating process. The larger study, under the leadership of Paul T. David, Director of Governmental Studies of the Institution, is planned for early publication under the title *The Politics of National Party Conventions*. As the research materials on television multiplied, it became increasingly clear that this subject should not be compressed into one chapter of the major volume as originally contemplated. Since the subject was both important and timely, it was decided to publish this treatment separately.

Dr. Thomson brings extensive experience to the field of communications research. He served during World War II with the Army and the Office of War Information as a psychological warfare planning officer, and served as Staff Director of the President's Communications Policy Board in 1950–51. He is the author of the volume, *Overseas Information Service of the United States Government*, published by Brookings in 1948.

A semi-final draft of the present book was reviewed by the Advisory Committee of distinguished scholars, serving as consultants to the Institution for the study of the presi-

v

dential nominating process. The committee includes: Arthur N. Holcombe, Chairman, Louis Brownlow, Richard S. Childs, Alexander Heard, Peter H. Odegard, Louise Overacker, and James K. Pollock. For the helpful suggestions of this committee, the author and the Institution are deeply indebted.

Paul T. David and Ralph M. Goldman of the Brookings staff assisted in developing the early plans for the study. There was extensive consultation with members of the staffs of the major networks, a number of federal agencies, the national party committees, several advertising agencies, and a number of political scientists and others who have carried on research on these matters. For this invaluable assistance, the author and the Institution are most grateful. Special thanks are due to Dr. Hugh M. Beville of the National Broadcasting Company, who provided special tabulations of television statistics and made available an unpublished study conducted by NBC; and the A. C. Nielsen Company, which provided special tabulations of audiences for 1952 political telecasts.

Finally, on behalf of the Institution, I wish to express grateful appreciation to The John Randolph Haynes and Dora Haynes Foundation of Los Angeles for its generous grants in 1953 and 1955 in support of the study of the presidential nominating process, of which the present volume is one of the results. The conclusions and recommendations of the study have been reached, however, wholly independently of the Haynes Foundation, which is not to be understood as approving or disapproving the views expressed in this and other volumes that will result from the investigation.

ROBERT D. CALKINS
President

February 1, 1956

Contents

Chapter VI

Chapter VII

Introduction

No ONE knows with any scientific exactitude what the impact of television has been on politics or what potentials it may hold for the future. It is certain, however, that the impact has already been considerable—on the practices of politicians, of communications industries, and of the people at large, if not on voting behavior as revealed by action on election day. It is also widely expected that the impact of television may increase, although the direction and power of its forces are not altogether clear. In 1952, many observers and participants claimed that television was having a pronounced effect on voters, candidates, and political parties. Certainly, it was conspicuous during the pre-convention preliminaries, at the conventions themselves, and during the campaigns that ended with the Eisenhower victory on November 4.

Nineteen hundred and fifty-two is taken as a year of special importance in the development of television, because it was the first year in which the national political conventions and the subsequent campaigning could be brought to a nationwide audience by that medium. The proceedings of both the Republican and the Democratic conventions were continuously broadcast over all four major television networks throughout the entire period of the convention sessions. About 18 million television receiving sets were in use at the time, most of them in homes. They were concentrated mainly in metropolitan areas of the East, the Middle West, and the Far West but were, nevertheless, available to about 40 per cent of all American families, including more than 50 per cent of the voters. Over half the American people watched at least part of the conventions on television. The impact of this experience on the choice of candidates was variously appraised, and estimates of the impact of television on the decision of the voters in November varied even more widely. Obviously, then, further research and analysis are indicated.

CHAPTER I

Television and Politics
Prior to 1952

A<small>LTHOUGH</small> television made its debut as a nationwide communications medium in the nominations and elections of 1952, in many respects it was not a complete
novelty at that time. Its practices as political reporter had
been developing slowly since 1940. The war interrupted its
progress, but it made considerable steps forward in the presidential election of 1948 and the off-year contests of 1950;
its development as a news medium was rooted firmly in the
practices of newspapers, wire services, magazines, radio, and
motion pictures.

Growth of the Medium

Television covered its first political conventions in 1940.
In that year, NBC and Philco brought both conventions to a
scattering of sets in New York and Philadelphia, showing
the keynote and nominating speeches, interviewing candidates and political experts, and picturing parades.[1] Some
40,000 to 100,000 people were estimated to have seen some
part of the proceedings, but there is no record that television
made any impact either on the convention procedure or the
election that followed. The medium had not grown beyond
the novelty stage.

In 1944, chiefly owing to the war, television had made little advance beyond 1940. There were nine stations telecasting to four eastern states and to parts of the Midwest and

[1] *Broadcasting* (May 15 and June 15, 1940).

3

Far West. An estimated 50,000 viewers saw the Republican convention on television, chiefly by film.[2] The difficulties of gearing indeterminate party procedure into the tight schedules of broadcasting were demonstrated in that year. In the Democratic convention, deadlocks in the credentials and the resolutions and platform committees disrupted the voting schedules. Voting for the nomination for Vice President completely dislocated radio network schedules.[3]

By July 1948, however, television was growing to the point where its political potentialities were more than foreshadowed. Although television was largely concentrated in the northeastern sector of the country,[4] an estimated 10 million people saw parts of the conventions on television that year. As yet, there was no commercial sponsorship of network coverage of activities on the convention floor.

The experience of 1948 offered fresh instruction to the parties, to other political participants, and to the press as a whole, as well as to the networks. Conscious of a new, larger, unfamiliar, and unpredictable audience, the parties tried to arrange convention business so that dull items would be disposed of during the day, and important events would fall during evening hours. Candidates, prohibited by custom from the freedom of the hall, found telecasts a useful and

[2] The same (June 26, 1944). NBC made two special films of the history of the Republican and the Democratic parties. These were shown prior to each convention, together with films of appropriate preliminaries—delegates arriving in the city, shots of the hall, and the like. NBC made a film in advance of Governor Warren's keynote speech and ran it simultaneously with the speech itself. During each convention, the networks shot film, flew it to the stations, and each evening showed half-hour edited versions of the events of the day and evening sessions preceding.

[3] *Broadcasting* (June 19, July 10, 17, and 24, 1944).

[4] There were 30 stations in 15 states (including the District of Columbia) in 18 metropolitan areas, with only three stations west of the Mississippi. The TV area then included 37 per cent of all United States homes. The states in which TV operated had 276 electoral votes, 606 votes in the Democratic convention and 587 votes in the Republican convention. For location of stations and the networks existing at that time, see *Television Digest*, TV Directory No. 4 (July 1, 1948). The count excludes Utah, where the state's first television station went on the air on July 1, 1948. There were 420,000 sets, mostly in homes—1 per cent of the United States total.

comprehensive means of following developments directly.[5] The press found television a useful tool for the same purposes.

Television was closely linked with press and radio, as the main radio networks made news personnel available for television news coverage, and joint coverage in partnership was worked out between Dumont and *Newsweek* and NBC and *Time-Life*.

The television networks originated their system of pooled broadcasts, apportioning the cost of covering the conventions among the eighteen East Coast stations. They also experimented with a variety of supplements to the pooled picture, providing exclusive reporting and news commentary. A good deal of effort was made to bring the viewer "news in depth," possibly to the detriment of detailed but unornamented presentation of the convention itself. And there were instances in which the networks treated an event in a light vein. Gilbert Seldes reports an instance in which a director for *Life*-NBC got southern delegates to add drama to their exit from the Democratic convention by coming to the NBC studios at the rear of the hall, tearing off their badges, and flinging them in a pile before the television camera; some time after the interviews were over the delegates returned and put their badges on again.[6]

Even in 1948, there were predictions that radio-television would change conventions drastically, robbing them of their spontaneity and altering traditional convention-hall atmosphere by loading the hall with strange equipment.

After the conventions, television grew rapidly. By the

[5] *Broadcasting-Telecasting* (June 28, 1948), pp. 21, 75.

[6] Gilbert Seldes, *The Great Audience* (1950), p. 207. Seldes, not always a friendly critic, commented: "The director who suggested the piece of business was not false to the meaning of the event, but he had illustrated the way in which the great instrument for conveying the simple truth can be subdued to the uses of accepted faking." (The same.) Thus Seldes does not question the accuracy of the camera, but asks the more searching question: What is the camera being accurate about?

time of the elections, there were 38 stations in operation. But on September 30, 1948, the Federal Communications Commission froze the receipt and processing of new applications for permits to construct stations, allowing the 70 then building to go ahead.[7] During the freeze, there was a maximum of 108 stations on the air.

The off-year elections of 1950 suggested the political potency of the new medium, which was used not only in Governor Dewey's famous marathon, but also in Senator Taft's campaign in Ohio.[8] The geography of the medium was still restricted to metropolitan areas, chiefly in the East and Far West, although there were stations in two thirds of the states. It was important in certain states, but the television medium had yet to demonstrate nationwide potentialities; and the great majority of politicians had yet to deal with television as an integral part of campaigning.

The freeze on new applications to build stations was maintained until April 1952, and not until July 11, 1952, did the FCC take action allowing new stations to go on the air.[9] The number of stations available to carry the conventions of 1952 had thus been stabilized at 108 for some time.[10]

[7] Lawrence P. Lessing, "The Television Freeze," *Fortune*, Vol. 40 (November 1949), pp. 123 ff. The freeze was required by technical considerations. The FCC had underestimated the amount of separation required to keep television stations from interfering unduly with one another. As the number of stations increased, both normal and special forms of interference grew. The most difficult seemed to be tropospheric interference. By mid-1948, reception was seriously hampered in many areas. (The same, p. 164.)

[8] Senator Taft's use of television in Ohio was managed by the Kudner advertising agency; the agency promptly associated the Senator's unprecedented margin of victory with his use of television. See *Broadcasting-Telecasting* (Aug. 4, 1952), p. 25. Kudner officials claimed that television enabled Senator Taft to reach millions rather than thousands, by foregoing some personal appearances but multiplying audiences for those he made.

[9] *Broadcasting-Telecasting* (July 14, 1952), p. 5.

[10] There seems to be no direct evidence to show that political pressure contributed to the lifting of the freeze in April of a presidential election year. This pressure may have been present, but due to the relatively low current estimate of the value of television to campaigning, it was not considered great. The FCC had been under severe pressure for a long time from the broadcasting industry to lift the freeze for

But the number of sets had greatly increased. At the time of the 1952 conventions, there were over 18 million sets, mostly in homes, aggregating 39 per cent of all homes in the United States. In areas that could receive television signals, 62 per cent of all homes had sets. Concentration of sets and stations in the metropolitan areas was still heavy, but the relative concentration in the northeastern states had been sharply reduced. There were outlets in 33 states (and the District of Columbia), 12 west of the Mississippi. The sparsely covered areas were in the Northwest and the South.[11]

Television service was far more concentrated than radio coverage, even in the political areas where both were found. Television was found in metropolitan areas, and in many of them there was only one station to carry programs originating locally or with any one of the four major networks. These stations perforce had to select from available fare, thus automatically determining the choice of the local viewer. He could see what there was to see on the one station, or nothing.

The maximum stretch of the political geography of television in mid-1952 is shown by the table on page 8, which classifies states by percentage of area covered by existing tele-

---

purely economic and competitive reasons. The issues related to the technology of transmission: interference both mutually among television transmitters and with other forms of broadcast service, including FM radio; and the economic competition between established stations in the Very High Frequency (VHF) spectrum band, and proposed stations in the Ultra High Frequency (UHF) band. In any case, the maintenance of the freeze until April 1952 meant that the politically significant television service for that year's campaign was substantially limited to stations in action on that date, because of the length of time required to build a station and get it on the air.

[11] Oregon, Nevada, Idaho, Wyoming, Montana, Colorado, North and South Dakota, and Maine had negligible coverage or none at all. A bit of Nebraska was served from Omaha. New Hampshire and Vermont got a little service from Massachusetts and New York. Kansas was served from Kansas City, Missouri. Arkansas got some signals from Memphis, Mississippi from Memphis and New Orleans, and South Carolina from Charlotte, North Carolina. (See map of Television in the United States, 1952, prepared July 15, 1952 by *Television Digest*. The service areas are based on 60-mile radius coverage of existing stations.) Although Denver, Colorado; Portland, Oregon; and Fresno, California, had no station outlets, they were served by closed-circuit television in hotels or theaters, and viewers could see the conventions at no expense to themselves. *Broadcasting-Telecasting* (June 30, 1952).

vision stations, and indicates their electoral votes and the
votes allocated to them in the Republican and Democratic
national conventions in 1952.

It is noteworthy that in only 15 states was more than half
the population living within range of television signals, but
these states cast 280 electoral votes, 631 votes in the Republican convention, and 618 votes in the Democratic convention
—just over half in each contest. More than one quarter of the
population lived within range of television in 28 states, controlling 410 electoral votes out of 531; 906 of 1,206 Republican National Convention votes; and 926 of 1,230 Democratic National Convention votes. Clearly, television as a
medium of political communication had the physical opportunity to play a powerful role in the nominations and elections of 1952.

POLITICAL GEOGRAPHY OF TELEVISION IN MID-1952

TV Density[a] (Per cent)	Number of States	1952 Electoral College Vote			1952 Convention Vote	
		Repub-lican	Demo-cratic	Total	Repub-lican	Demo-cratic
100.............	3[b]	28	0		74	66
75–100..........	6	140	0	168	316	296
50–75...........	6	112	0	280	241	256
25–50..........	13	88	42	410	275	308
1–25...........	13	43	47	500	87	204
0.............	7[c]	31	0	531	113	100
TOTAL.......	48	442	89	531	1,206	1,230

[a] Per cent population in TV area.
[b] Plus the District of Columbia.
[c] Plus five territories and possessions.

Emerging Estimates of Strategy
and Significance, 1951–52

It is difficult, indeed, even with the advantage of hindsight,
to make out accurately the emerging attitudes toward the

relation of television to politics that the industry, the parties, and the various candidates for the 1952 presidential nominations held late in 1951. The industry was moving toward a profitable basis and was eager for various means of increasing its public. Coverage of the political conventions furnished a readily available means to this end, for which pre-convention campaigning of the candidates would serve as an appropriate precursor. The conventions themselves were natural vehicles for demonstrating the contributions of television to public enlightenment or entertainment, or both. The television industry, in its advertising and public statements, widely hailed the conventions as the greatest political show on earth, a special event of magistral proportions, which would be brought to the people in vividness and detail as never before. The public service elements were not neglected; television would produce the best informed and most interested electorate in American political history.

Party attitudes on when and how to use television, or at any rate toward accepting it, were somewhat milder than would be expected in retrospect. Committee professionals concerned with radio and television were well aware of the potentialities and limitations of television, but it is not apparent that all the senior men of the parties were equally impressed. Both Republicans and Democrats produced handbooks on how candidates could use television and other media most effectively in 1952, and both committees counseled party members to enlist the help of advertising agencies in doing so. The Democratic publicity division told its speakers and delegation chairmen that television would have a vital effect on the party, the chances of candidates, and the attitudes of the people toward the party and the election. The division issued the first of a long series of warnings concerning the ubiquitous eye of television and urged that conventions must now be geared to television.

Opinion was widespread both in the broadcasting trade

press and among television officials that Democrats were more inclined than Republicans to favor television and to turn it to their purposes. Conflicting with this view, however, is the fact that the Republican Congressional Committee took the initiative in putting television at the disposal of campaigning Republican congressmen in 1950, and maintained this initiative in the years following.[12]

Candidate attitudes varied, as did opinion and practice within the local party organizations. The Taft group was widely believed by the television industry to be against television. Apparently, instances occurred in which persons surrounding the Senator were difficult to deal with if not openly hostile to the medium, thinking that it put their candidate at a disadvantage. The Senator himself was far less pessimistic, possibly owing to his experience in 1950. Prior to 1952 the Taft group had clearly wanted political time—especially time to answer Democrats who had appeared on television. The Dewey group was openly in favor of exploiting television to the fullest. The Governor had used the medium both in the 1948 campaign and in his races for the governorship; he had worked hard to overcome an initial appearance of aloofness, to train his television voice and manner, and to learn other tricks of the television trade. He took every opportunity to use television—and the behavior of the Taft faction—to give the appearance of candor to his intra-party

[12] Under the guidance of Robert Humphreys (later in charge of publicity for the Republican National Committee), the Congressional Committee made five five-minute television films for use of Republican candidates for Congress. The committee provided standard scripts, direction, printed visual aids, and other promotional materials. The committee told candidates how to get time on TV, urging the purchase of spots. They also provided slide films. In 1951, the Republicans opened a studio on Capitol Hill to make television films at low cost for Republican congressmen. This was later taken over with congressional support and run on a bipartisan basis.

According to Humphreys, the Republicans also used television with telling effect in special elections in 1951 and 1952. In the first year, the Republicans upset a normally Democratic district in St. Louis, and in 1952, in Dayton, Ohio, the Republicans took another seat away from the Democrats. In both campaigns, "television helped."

moves and to his pre-convention campaign for General Eisenhower.

General Eisenhower's attitude toward television was two-fold. From the standpoint of use of the medium by the party, he interposed no objection to plans proposed by national committee specialists and was always willing to appear on the screen on appropriate occasions, but he was not favorably disposed toward the use of visual aids or gimmicks.[13] He felt most at home and was most effective in very informal situations.

Senator Kefauver had been made into a national figure overnight by television coverage of his crime investigations. He and most of the other Democratic candidates for the nomination eagerly accepted attentions of television.

[13] Interview with Robert Humphreys, November 1955. CBS's David Schoenbrun of the SHAPE correspondents' association, has testified to the difficulty of persuading the General to make television appearances during his SHAPE days. CBS Press Release (July 16, 1952). The President's early diffidence persisted for a long time. Various television newsmen and officials, commenting on his appearances during the 1952 campaign and up to the fall of 1954, have reported his continuing sense of discomfort when before the cameras, despite intensive professional coaching. They report that the President has said the medium makes him feel like an actor, and he isn't one. Despite this, the President has made increasingly effective appearances, notable among which were his reports to the nation apropos of the Geneva Conference in the summer of 1955.

CHAPTER II

Television and the National Conventions of 1952

Long before the 1952 conventions opened, the potential candidates were jockeying for position, and the networks were laying their plans both for physical installations and for programing. The story of these developments and their results falls into three phases: preparation; pre-convention television operations; and television coverage of the conventions themselves.

Preparations

The political parties, the networks and stations, and the potential commercial sponsors all had a direct interest in the preparations for television coverage of the 1952 conventions. Although the candidates also had an obvious interest, their participation will be considered in the section below, under pre-convention television. The interests to be served required not only the manipulation of large physical items—convention halls, hotel space, transmission equipment—but also the intermeshing of related and sometimes antithetical interests and goals. The parties were interested in a smooth staging of an important quadrennial event and the placement of their candidates and programs in a favorable light. The networks were interested both in public service and in financial gain—gain not only in terms of revenue from sponsors to offset the very heavy out-of-pocket expenses, but from demonstration of the value of the medium and from sale of equipment, and thus from expansion of the base for the economic future of television. The commercial sponsors were interested in securing both an enhanced reputation for public service and an opportunity to demonstrate their wares to an enormous audience. Identification with the political events of the conventions served all these ends, in varying fashion and degrees.[1]

The networks commenced their planning for convention coverage as early as May 1951.[2] Top executives and engineers spent many man-hours in making arrangements for specifications and allocation of facilities for pool coverage. Many more hours were spent in four cities in the joint negotiations with the parties over the convention site and various conditions prerequisite for satisfactory operations. The networks conducted these negotiations through a committee under the chairmanship of Thomas Velotta, Vice President of ABC. This committee dealt with the chairmen of the two national committees, their public relations directors, and their specialists for radio and television.

The networks and the committees considered the location of the convention city, the selection of the hall in the city, the question of who should bear expenses incident to coverage, the issue of whether or not the conventions would be sponsored, and, if sponsored, the specifications for determining an appropriate sponsor.

The advent of television as a major medium affected for the first time the choice of convention city by both parties.

[1] This viewpoint was suggested by Riddick Lawrence, Director of Promotion, Planning, and Development for NBC, in a speech reported in *Advertising Age* (Sept. 15, 1952), p. 14. After summarizing a study of convention viewing done for NBC by Advertest, Lawrence pointed out that television could make up a deficiency in current advertising by selling not the end product, but what is behind the product. Television can do this "by identifying the advertiser with great culture and entertainment and by showing, through the camera, 'the ideas and principles which make your company tick.' "

[2] See testimony of Frank Stanton, President of CBS, before Senate Subcommittee No. 2 on Communications, *Status of UHF and Multiple Ownership of TV Stations*, Hearings before the Senate Committee on Interstate and Foreign Commerce, 83 Cong. 2 sess., p. 991.

In 1944, both committees had little choice of cities because of wartime travel restrictions and other considerations. By 1948, there seemed to be other and equally persuasive reasons for the two committees to join in selection of Philadelphia as the convention city. But in 1952, the sheer physical magnitude of the planned requirements for television coverage persuaded both parties to choose the same city, and in it a location that would favor effective television operation. The Republican convention management group had almost decided to meet in the Chicago stadium, but after strong arguments from the network representatives (plus some prompt decisions by the representative of the stockyards), the Chicago amphitheatre was chosen. Adequate adjacent indoor space for bulky equipment and a promise of air-conditioning turned the favor of the networks to the amphitheatre.[3]

The network problem with respect to the location of the city also included the factors of time and technology. It was preferable to have a city in the Central time belt, so that the difference in hours of viewing from coast to coast would affect least the convenience of the majority of viewers. It was necessary to have the conventions in a city in which it was possible to originate television programs—a far more restricted choice in 1952 than today. Finally, it was important to be in a place in which the logistical effort and cost of moving people and equipment to cover the event would be reasonable.

The issue who should bear the cost of installations was tied up with the issue of "sponsorship" of the conventions.[4] In

[3] See statement of Sig Mickelson of CBS, in a press release dated Nov. 12, 1951. Mickelson pointed out that television was the only medium to be represented at the meetings of the national committees held to select the convention site.

[4] The terms "sponsor" and "sponsorship" are used here and elsewhere in this monograph in the sense in which the usage has become common in the radio and television industries. The terminology itself tends to create issues, as it carries implications that go far beyond what is normally contemplated in the purchase and sale of advertising time or space. On development of the notion and its relation to broadcasting, see Charles Siepmann, *Radio, Television and Society* (1950), pp. 10, 14, 48–55, 182; and Gilbert Seldes, *The Great Audience* (1950).

1948, the national committees had paid the cost of installing studio space in the hall, with the networks paying for special equipment, in consideration of the fact that the networks were not seeking commercial sponsorship for the conventions but were carrying them as a public service. In mid-1951, the networks were proposing to seek commercial sponsors, on the ground that they could thereby defray at least part of their expenses and give better coverage to the event as a whole. The committees, aware of this intention, examined the problem from their own standpoint and proceeded to the negotiations. The representatives of the parties first tried to get some of the sponsorship fees, and later insisted that the networks should bear the full cost of installing and housing their equipment, inasmuch as they would be paid for broadcasting the event. The networks at first held out for a continuation of the 1948 arrangement, on the ground that they would be spending much more than they would take in. Later the networks agreed to take on the cost of installation insofar as they obtained sponsors. As all four networks did obtain sponsors, the ground was cut from under their position, and in the end, they paid for their installation costs.

The issue of sponsorship had other aspects of greater importance than its effect on the cost of installation. The networks wanted to keep a free hand to make the best financial arrangements possible, and were loath to allow an outside agency to come between them and any potential sponsor or his agents. The parties wished to be sure that the sponsorship would be appropriate, that pressure would not be brought to bear on the conduct and organization of the conventions, and that the activities of the sponsor would be clearly dissociated from those of the parties.

The networks and the parties agreed on a code to regulate these matters for radio as well as for television. This code provided that the two major parties had no objections to commercial sponsorship of network television and radio coverage of the 1952 conventions, subject to the following conditions:

A. The type of sponsor shall be approved by the political parties.

B. Commercial messages may be made only during recesses or during periods of long pauses during the actual convention proceedings.

C. Commercial messages must meet the highest standards of dignity, good taste, and length.

D. No commercial announcement may be made from the floor of the convention.

E. There shall be a disclaimer made at the beginning and end of each broadcast period. This disclaimer shall make perfectly clear two points: (1) that the client is sponsoring the network's coverage of the event; (2) that sponsorship by —— Company of the —— network's coverage does not imply in any manner an endorsement of the product by the political party. All commercial announcements shall be written, programmed, and delivered in such a way as to be clearly and completely separated from convention proceedings, political parties, issues and personalities.[5]

The networks insisted on the letter of the code providing that the parties had the power to approve only a *type* of sponsor, not any particular sponsor. They agreed not to suggest merchandisers of laxatives, deodorants, liquor, or similar products as sponsors. They also agreed to notify the committees in advance of the sponsors actually being chosen. As a matter of fact, CBS and NBC had announced their sponsors well before the agreed text of the code was made public.[6]

The difficulties inherent in the concepts and terminology of "sponsorship" remained and were accepted by the party managers, aside from the provisions in the code making it

[5] The code was agreed to among the American Broadcasting Company, the Columbia Broadcasting System, Dumont, Liberty Broadcasting System, Mutual Broadcasting System, and the National Broadcasting Company on the one hand; on the other the agreement was approved for the political parties by the Republican and Democratic national committee chairmen. The text of the code is given in press releases by the Democratic and Republican national committees dated Mar. 6, 1952.

[6] CBS announced on Dec. 28, 1951, that Westinghouse would sponsor the conventions and the campaign coverage. NBC announced Philco's sponsorship on Jan. 2, 1952. Although the code had been under discussion prior to this point, it was not formally announced until Mar. 6, 1952.

clear that the sponsorship applied to the coverage rather than to the event itself.

The networks recognized from the outset that the conventions should not be used as a backdrop for the "hard sell" and promised the committees that this would not be done. But both network and party negotiators knew that the actual presentation of the conventions and the use of advertising in connection therewith would be decided in part at the point of outlet—the local station—and the networks could speak definitely only for those that they owned. No matter what the networks might promise or the committees demand, there was always the possibility that the independently owned local station would cut off the network signal and run spot materials, either political or commercial, of its own. There was no easy way that either the networks or the political parties could monitor or control this effectively. But it could be assumed that the interest of the local station worked toward keeping its coverage in line with the tone and spirit of network material. No flagrant cases of violation of the code by local stations appeared.

The networks insisted on complete editorial freedom to decide how they would televise the convention. Hence no agreements with the parties were made concerning the extent to which the networks would devote attention to events on the floor, as compared to other events relating to the whole convention process.

The committees were jealous of their control over the proceedings of the convention, and there were many misgivings expressed publicly and privately that the advertising agencies for the sponsors might try to manage convention proceedings in order to put on a more sprightly show, or one better suited to the particular interest of the sponsor.

The committees tried to prevent television coverage by portable equipment used on the floor of the hall itself. The effect of this, so far as the type of coverage was concerned, was largely nullified by the enterprise of one network, which installed a camera with a long-range lens in its control booth. The other networks quickly copied this example. Thus, in effect, each network could transmit either the agreed-on "pool" picture, or its own picture from the hall itself.

A continuing problem requiring negotiation between the networks and each party management involved the relative allocation of space at the convention hall to radio, television, motion pictures, and the press. The needs of television were considerably greater and more complicated than those of the other media, although television required comparatively little space in the hall itself. A certain amount of platform space on the floor, so located as to give a good picture of the speaker's platform, was all that was needed there. By placing cameras at the sides and back of the hall and by using long-range lenses, the television networks could easily focus upon any-thing in the hall not available from the floor platform, such as an interview with a caucus or prominent manager or dele-gate on the floor. The requirements for facilities and person-nel were summarized by *Fortune* as follows:

TV transported over $4 million worth of equipment to Chicago. CBS moved in twenty tons of gear, including the equipment to operate a CBS-NBC-ABC camera pool, twenty cameras of its own, three mobile units, walkie-talkies, control panels, hundreds of miles of wire and cable, and a repair shop. . . . To man the operation, CBS had some 300 news-men and technicians in Chicago. NBC's and ABC's operations were comparable.[7]

The problem was not how to accommodate television and yet seat all delegates and alternates (about 3,000 individuals), so much as it was to seat the host of guests, of varying de-grees of political importance, who, since the time of Lincoln, have provided the familiar backdrop to convention proceed-

---

[7] "TV After Chicago," *Fortune* (September 1952), pp. 86, 210.

ings. Television naturally wanted locations that would allow the best viewing angles. But the committees were reluctant to give up platform space at points in the hall where delegation seating might be diminished, and booth arrangements in the galleries reduced potential visitor space. The committees had not yet come to a sufficient appreciation of the political value of television to grant it a large space allocation in the face of strong competition from other press media and other traditional demands for space in the convention hall. Nor had television yet demonstrated that the picture it provides can give far better comprehension and coverage of the essence of the convention than does a seat on the floor or in the gallery, thus reducing the demand for space by guests or by other press media.

The newspaper and periodical press, with its long history of association with the parties and its demonstrated political worth, was given ample space—one-third of the floor. This proved to be more than was actually needed, since many members of the working press made little use of the area provided for them at that location. The requirements of radio were not large, and were taken care of jointly with those for television. Newsreels presented a special problem since they required brilliant lighting, as they had in previous conventions.

Negotiations between the networks and the commercial sponsors or their advertising agencies did not involve the national committees to a great extent. They became seriously concerned only in connection with the proposed sponsorship of Dumont coverage by *Life*. This situation arose in the summer of 1951, with Mr. Henry Luce's announcement that he was interested in sponsoring convention coverage.[8] The possible political consequences of a politically interested commercial sponsorship of the conventions were immediately

[8] *New York Times* (July 13, 1951), p. 24.

recognized, although there was little or no public discussion of it for some months. It remained an issue under the surface, however, and some Republican party factions, and Democratic party officials generally, did not look favorably upon any such sponsorship. This possibility undoubtedly underlay the negotiations between the networks and the party committees relating to sponsorship. But the issue did not receive much public attention until the announcement by Dumont, in January 1952, that an agreement with *Life* was being negotiated for joint coverage of both conventions. *Life* was to be present in a purely reportorial capacity, and was to contribute to the coverage of the event its technical and research facilities, as well as its journalistic talent. This announcement immediately called forth expressions of misgivings from Taft Republicans and some Democrats, on the ground that the publisher of *Life* had already announced his support for Eisenhower.[9] The proposed arrangement was not consummated. Dumont, which could offer at best only a limited array of stations, was sponsored by Westinghouse jointly with CBS.

The ultimate network sponsors were politically neutral makers of electrical equipment or prominent manufacturers of television sets: Westinghouse, Philco, and Admiral. Network negotiations with sponsors were carried on informally, with a minimum of written agreement. In no case did a sponsor arrange for coverage of the conventions only. The agreements were "package deals," calling for both radio and television coverage of the conventions, the intervening period of the campaign, and the reporting of returns on election night.[10] The agreements by NBC and ABC with their sponsors required the sponsor to pay for a minimum number of

[9] See *Radio Daily* (Jan. 23 and 29, 1952).

[10] See, for example, the NBC press release of Jan. 2, 1952, announcing the general terms of its arrangement with Philco for coverage of the 1952 conventions and election.

hours, while the network agreed to cover the whole convention at no additional cost to the sponsor if the convention overran the agreed minimum period. CBS made a more prescient agreement with Westinghouse, in which the payment would be adjusted to the total number of hours broadcast.

Pre-Convention Television

The relationship of television to the presidential nominating process during the period prior to the conventions themselves is threefold: television presents candidates for the nomination, declared or undeclared, and may help to create them; television focuses attention on the convention as a "special event" through its various ways of describing and analyzing a political institution; and television covers the vital moves of the political parties made prior to the convention itself—in particular, the work of the national committees and their subcommittees.

The more astute and enterprising of the admitted candidates and their managers made every effort during the pre-convention period to get time on television. They sought spots on quiz-shows, panel discussions, "Meet the Press," and so forth. The major figures were sought by the networks and stations in return. But not all candidates, active or available, were eager for the attention of television; General Eisenhower was a notable case in point. The telecast of his homecoming to Abilene was unfortunate, to say the least. He brought with him no avidity for television; rain, discomfort, and dreariness accentuated the candidate's unwillingness all too clearly. Many viewers were impressed with what appeared to be a lack of presence and vitality. But the next morning, at his press conference, he recouped, but not because of the cunning of his managers. They put up strong barriers to television coverage, which were overcome only by the persistence of the networks.[11] Even after the event, his great success in projecting an impression of vigor and clarity was more convincing to his managers than to him.[12]

Television gave considerable attention to the state primaries and conventions, carrying them not only as news but as full-fledged special events. CBS, for example, sent the Douglas Edwards news show to New Hampshire a month before the election, to sample opinion among Democratic and Republican leaders. Camera teams followed Senators Taft and Kefauver around the state, providing film reports of their campaigns early in March. On the days immediately preceding the voting on March 11, Edwards interviewed Taft and Adams. The election itself was covered on the spot. Similar coverage was given by CBS and the other networks to the Minnesota, Wisconsin, and Nebraska nomination campaigns and to the state conventions. These were covered both as news and as special events of local and immediate as well as emerging national importance.

Station logs and network records provide information about what was covered and where it was telecast in this pre-convention period, but who watched and with what effect seems now to be lost beyond the point of precise measurement. It does appear, however, in sharp contrast to the ex-

[11] Jerry Walker, "Only White House Doors Will Stop TV Now," *Editor and Publisher* (June 14, 1952), p. 54. Walker reported that Robert Mullen, who was handling Eisenhower's public relations at the time, did not wish to evict the television crews who set up for line coverage despite strong intimations they were not welcome. The press resented TV's presence for two reasons: (1) pressmen complained that in a televised press conference they were unwilling, unpaid actors unable to press a line of questioning; and (2) they were inescapably scooped by television. (Under so-called "Washington rules," no newspaperman can leave the press conference to file his story until the conference is officially ended. Live television naturally reports the event as it develops.)

[12] For many months afterward industry people reported his reluctance to go before the cameras. For a later favorable appraisal of the President's effective television performance under conditions of relaxed informality, see the note by Roger Kennedy in the *New Republic* (May 30, 1955), commenting on the telecast of Dulles reporting to Eisenhower on May 17.

perience of early conventions, that modern communications had provided many delegates and managers with a far more complete docket of information, and with more matured attitudes toward personalities and issues developed during the pre-convention period, than they previously enjoyed before the convention itself had assembled and political soundings could be taken at the site.

Television was just beginning to make a prominent contribution to this process in 1952. The total effect of television reporting was still limited by the small number and distribution of existing stations; many of those on the air in July had just begun operations. Others that had been operating for a longer time had concentrated more on local topics than on national news, and were not yet geared either by transmission facilities or editorial experience to do a first-class job of national coverage, even when the material was available by film or remote pick-up.

Although general observation suggests that television as a whole provided reasonably adequate time for political purposes in the pre-convention campaigning, it is doubtful whether any of the candidates themselves (with the exceptions of Eisenhower and Stevenson) felt they got as much time on television as they would like. Access to the screen is necessarily limited on any of the three avenues: purchased time, public service time, or appearance on shows. Purchased time is expensive. Public service time is limited by the policies of the networks, the public position of the candidates, and regulations of the Federal Communications Commission. The number of appropriate shows—established shows like "Meet the Press," "Town Meeting of the Air," or special ones like "Presidential Timber" or "Where Do You Stand," for example—are few and offer room for only a limited number of potential or declared candidates. The total of public service time and news-show or panel time provided far more opportunity to candidates than bought time. One reason for this was that several of the candidates—notably the governors—could use television regularly and effectively in reporting (albeit to a localized audience) on the problems and progress of their offices.

Access was further limited by the interpretation placed by the networks and the individual stations on their responsibilities under the Federal Communications Act. It should be said in passing that these responsibilities are those of the stations, as it is they, and not the networks as such, that hold the license to use specified portions of the radio spectrum and that must perform duties arising under the act. These responsibilities are twofold, and arise both under Section 315 of the act, governing access to the air of candidates for office, and under the general standard that stations holding licenses under the act must provide balanced treatment of public issues as part of a well-rounded service to the public. This standard is considered by the Federal Communications Commission in determining whether a station is meeting the test of service to the public interest, convenience, and necessity written specifically into the act.

Because the number of people who can qualify as candidates under Section 315 is very large, the networks faced (and face) a serious problem in making their facilities available for political purposes without jeopardizing the over-all quality and balance of their programs, their income from commercial time sales, and their position before the FCC as providers of an adequate diet of public service programs. It is probable that many requests for network time (or local station time as well) were tactfully discouraged in the pre-convention period, usually on grounds that the candidate or his views were not sufficiently well known to warrant appearance on the air.

But in 1952, one determined candidate illustrated what

could be done to get time on the television and radio networks. William R. Schneider approached CBS, asking for free time to expound his views on the air. This was denied on grounds that he was not well enough known, nor were his views of sufficient public interest. But Schneider filed as candidate for the Republican nomination in both New Hampshire and Oregon, thus making himself a nationwide candidate. Then he renewed his request, this time under Section 315, pointing out that both Senator Taft and General Eisenhower had been carried on a network program. He took the matter to the FCC, which ruled that he was entitled to the protection of Section 315. CBS accordingly gave him two network half-hours free. Schneider was heard over eight television stations on June 20, 1952 from 10:30 to 11:00 P.M. EDST, and over 97 radio stations on June 19, 1952 at the same hour.[13]

The consequences of the Schneider case are compounded because under FCC rules the meaning of "candidates" is not limited to the candidates for nomination by the major parties. Time must be provided on an equal basis for all, and in 1952 there were eighteen bona fide parties.[14] Networks must also consider independent candidates who qualify as candidates under FCC regulations.

A study reported in 1952 indicated that the majority of television stations did not give free political time, and restricted access to the medium in various ways. Stations do not ordinarily solicit purchase of time for political purposes.

[13] Letter from the FCC to CBS dated May 28, 1952; and testimony of Richard S. Salant, Executive Vice President, CBS, before the Senate Subcommittee on Privileges and Elections, April 1955 (CBS, mimeo., no date); letter to the writer from William C. Ackerman, Director (Reference Department) CBS, Oct. 14, 1955.

[14] Aside from the Democratic, Republican, and Socialist parties, there were the American party, the American Rally, the Christian Nationalist party, Church of God Bible party, Constitution party, Greenback party, Poor Man's party, Progressive party, Prohibition party, Republimerican party, Socialist Labor party, Socialist Worker's party, Spiritual party, Vegetarian party, and Washington Peace party.

Nearly half the television stations polled (thirty-three of which responded) restricted time for political broadcasting during campaigns, and over half (59.8 per cent) between campaigns.[15]

An innovation in network and station practice took place in the winter of 1951–52, with the announcement that the stations would sell time to candidates for the nomination prior to the national conventions. Previously the stations had not sold time for this purpose, but made it available on a public service basis. NBC and ABC announced that as of January 15, 1952, they would sell time to any legally qualified candidate or to persons speaking in behalf of such a candidate.[16]

After preliminary expressions of dudgeon from candidates, managers, and commentators[17] some time was actually bought. Prior to the Republican convention, the NBC network alone carried nine broadcasts for various Eisenhower sponsors, totaling seven and one-half hours of broadcast time at a gross time charge of $118,938.73. These broadcasts originated from New York, Washington, D. C., Boston, Detroit, and Denver. They were sponsored by the Eisenhower Bandwagon Committee, the Citizens for Eisenhower Committee, and the Michigan for Eisenhower Committee.[18] No time was bought from the network by Democratic candidates or sponsors during this period. There was an abortive effort made by the Russell for President Headquarters to schedule a program for July 14, but the broadcast was canceled.

---

[15] *Broadcasting-Telecasting* (Oct. 20, 1952), p. 28, summarizing the work of Richard H. Hall.

[16] See the "1952 NBC Political Broadcast Procedures," p. 1 (litho., no date); ABC press release (Jan. 14, 1952).

[17] See, for example, Gilbert Seldes, "Politics—Televised and Sponsored," *Saturday Review of Literature* (Mar. 15, 1952).

[18] Based on tabulations furnished by the National Broadcasting Company, September 1954.

Network policies governing purchase of time for broadcasts by candidates for the nomination were the same as those
that governed subsequent political broadcasting by or in behalf of the nominees of the parties. These policies included
cash payment in advance; equal treatment for opposing
candidates for the same office; restriction of facilities to the
candidate himself or to persons or groups speaking on his
behalf with his knowledge and consent; payment at regular
time-rates, plus additional charges for any further costs incident to cancellation of commercial programs; and com-
pliance with required formulas for signing on and off programs designed to identify properly the sponsorship of the
political program.[19]

The pre-convention role of the national committees was
understandably limited. Fairness to all potential candidates in
the party prohibits exclusive support of the candidacy of any
one person except when a president in office is a candidate to
succeed himself; the national party organization awaits the
decision of the convention. During this period, it makes arrangements for party publicity during and after the convention and renders general services to party candidates; it offers
advice on obtaining television time and using the medium effectively, and provides campaign materials of general applicability.

During the weeks preceding the conventions of 1952, all
four major networks devoted a large amount of attention to
the developing campaign for the nomination and to the forthcoming events of the conventions themselves. This pre-convention coverage was carried partly as a public service, and
partly as a special adaptation of existing shows dealing with
news and public affairs. NBC provided thirty-six hours of
special pre-convention programing, coming as a logical out-
growth of the network's reports on the presidential primary

[19] "1952 NBC Political Broadcast Procedures."

elections and state conventions, and leading up to the national conventions. These programs included biographies of the leading candidates, explanations of the mechanics of the conventions, and reviews of the Philadelphia conventions held in 1948. The network news program "Today" was originated from Chicago all through the month of July, and devoted major attention to the conventions themselves. The program "We the People" carried a thirteen-week series on the race for the presidential nominations. This series included live interviews with candidates and other prominent personalities, films, animated cartoons, and news commentary and analysis.[20]

The Columbia Broadcasting System scheduled 230 broadcasts in connection with the two conventions, with 66 special programs. Like NBC, the CBS network shifted many of its regularly scheduled weekly programs to Chicago, notably "Capitol Cloakroom" and "People's Platform."[21]

The American Broadcasting Company televised nine special events programs between July 4 and 8 covering the forthcoming convention, and supplemented its television coverage with twelve special events radio broadcasts.[22] Dumont contributed the notable "Author Meets the Critic" series, featuring candidates Stassen, Kefauver, and Taft on successive weeks in February.

On July 1, as the Republican National Committee moved into Chicago, television was already there making final preparations for covering the convention itself. But the most dramatic operating issues arose over covering the national committee even before the convention started. When the national committee convened for its first session, it found television, uninvited and not having asked permission in advance, preparing to cover the session. The first move of the com-

[20] *Broadcasting-Telecasting* (June 30, 1952), p. 37.
[21] Statement of Richard S. Salant, cited above.
[22] *Broadcasting-Telecasting* (June 30, 1952), p. 36.

mittee was to suggest a shift to another room, less crowded and cooler. Television prepared to follow, but the committee refused access. This posed an immediate challenge to television officials and newsmen; they knew the importance of the proceedings—especially those dealing with credentials—and made every effort to gain entry to them. Presidents of the networks sent telegrams to the committee asking for reconsideration of the ban against cameras and microphones—a ban that also cut out the newsreel cameras. They asked for rights equal with those of any other press medium to be present, and pointed out that television coverage need not disturb the conduct of the meeting.

The immediate result was to precipitate a factional struggle within the committee. The Taft faction, possessing a numerical majority and distrusting television, dragged its feet. The Dewey faction clamored for full television coverage. On a 60–40 vote, television and newsreel cameras were excluded, and direct press coverage was limited in effect to the paper-and-pencil requirement enforced in Congress.[23]

The ban stayed in effect until the convention met. This did not mean that radio was wholly excluded, however. CBS found a permanent line, used for dance music, installed in the meeting room, and used it to make tape recordings of important parts of the session. Within twenty minutes after recording, CBS went on the air with a thirty-minute program of the hotly contested debate in the national committee over seating the Texas delegation.[24]

Mounting pressure over exclusion of television from the committee sessions forced early consideration of access to the meetings of the convention committees. When the cre-

[23] The committee's decision to exclude television from direct coverage of its proceedings did not stop one network (NBC) from trying to picture events from a floor above. NBC finally did camera "spots" from a position outside the Boulevard Room of the convention hotel with interviews and reports from its reporters. This coverage was maintained from the time the committee met until it adjourned. Letter from William McAndrew, November 1955.

[24] *Broadcasting-Telecasting* (July 14, 1952), p. 36.

dentials committee of the convention met on Tuesday morning, it decided unanimously to open its proceedings to television and newsreels. The trade press crowed over the victory.[25] Once this decision was taken, Senator Taft issued a
statement repudiating the actions of his supporters; but it
was too late to eradicate the impression, already widespread,
owing to the efforts of the industry and to the Dewey faction, that the Taft forces wanted to shield their operations
from wide public inspection.[26]

Convention Television

Physical and programing arrangements for televising the
conventions were elaborately planned in advance. Cameras
were placed at the sides and back of the hall, from which
most activities in the area could be covered. But the Republican managers were unwilling to cut into delegate space and
did not allow camera placement that would afford a head-on
picture of the rostrum itself. As pointed out earlier, coverage
from the fixed cameras was supplemented by cameras each
network brought into its booth and equipped with long-range
lenses. These gave each network considerable choice of what
picture from the hall it could select. The various networks
had stressed in preliminary preparations coverage by portable television equipment that could roam the floor and the
hall.[27] This was to be augmented by radio walkie-talkies.

Basic coverage from the fixed cameras was to be pooled,
and a single director agreed on by the networks was put in

[25] *Editor and Publisher* (July 12, 1952), p. 69.
[26] Much of this story is told, from the industry's viewpoint, in *Broadcasting-
Telecasting* (July 7, 1952), pp. 33 ff.
[27] See, for example, the NBC press release of Jan. 2, 1952, announcing that Philco
would sponsor NBC convention-election coverage. This release quoted Philco's
Executive Vice President James H. Carmine that RCA "creepie-peepies" would be
at the convention for the first time.

charge. This director, Robert Doyle, worked from a central television booth from which he could control the activities of various cameramen covering proceedings on the floor or platform and could thus get the picture he wanted for the pool wire. Doyle had full authority to select this picture, with benefit of comment and criticism from the television directors of the participating networks. His choice was available to all four networks. But each network could decide at any time to cut away from the pooled picture and provide "side bar" programs, interviews, and the like.

There were no agreements between the networks and the convention management or the parties as to the precise form coverage would take. The underlying expectation was that attention would be centered on proceedings in the hall itself. There is no evidence of any discussion whether the networks should be bound to cover proceedings in the hall, no matter what else was going on.

The basic pattern of coverage planned by the networks for both conventions was simple. Their intention was to center attention on floor events from the time the convention opened each day until it recessed, filling the recesses with analysis and commentary, preparing the viewers for resumption by recapitulations, and staying with the conventions until they closed each night. This basic pattern would be interrupted by news comment and analysis, with interviews and with items of human interest and entertainment value originating both in the convention hall and elsewhere in the city. Stations carrying the convention were to make station-break announcements and carry spot advertisements at appropriate times, although it was hoped they would not seriously interrupt the thread of the convention story. The networks would also insert their commercials on behalf of their sponsors at appropriate moments. This gavel-to-gavel pattern was supplemented by covering such important preliminaries as meetings of the committees of the convention during the morning.[28] Variations in such preparatory coverage and supplementary material resulted in slightly different total hours of coverage given the convention event as a whole by each network.

Concentration on the floor proceedings of the convention as told in debates, formal addresses, committee reports, and other proceedings was largely adhered to by the networks during the Republican convention. This concentration may have been somewhat at the expense of coverage of committee proceedings and other off-the-floor events when they occurred simultaneously.[29] The networks began using a number of devices peculiar to television during the Republican convention: superimposing party symbols on the screen, cutting pictures of the commentator into the convention picture; and marking prominent personalities with circles or arrows. During the Democratic convention, periods of slow movement during the second and third days, coupled with the necessarily decreasing novelty of the event, prodded cameramen and editors to increase their use of trick devices and to search for special human interest material.

Search for novel devices and human interest shots during the 1952 conventions signaled an important problem in television coverage of the conventions. While the picture might have seemed dull to the average viewer, because the full significance of developments was not immediately apparent to him, these proceedings were not by any means dull to

[28] NBC, for example, carried special convention reports on "Today" (7–10 a.m.); a special convention show (9–10 a.m. EST) called "Convention Call"; the daily "Camel News Caravan"; plus a special series of "Meet the Press." All of these were outside of convention sessions. Letter from William McAndrew, November 1955.

[29] The difficulties of the networks in providing outside coverage were somewhat greater during the Republican convention than during the Democratic. On the second day of the earlier session, NBC had to carry the previously-contracted-for All-Star game; one of the speakers that day who did not appear on television live was Senator McCarthy. The same.

interested party activists. The question remains whether television commentators could have done a more adequate job of keeping viewers informed of the probable meaning of what was going on. The Republican controversies did not present quite the same problem as did the Democratic arguments, because their conflicts had greater inherent and apparent interest for independents and non-party people, both because the conflicts were more directly linked to the candidates and because the Republican winner was more likely to win the election.

The Republicans did little to adapt their proceedings to television or to coach the various delegates in television dress and manners. This may have resulted from inertia, from inexperience, or from a judgment that such exhortations would not do much good anyway once the pressure was on. The Democrats, however, announced great plans for turning television to full account—plans that did not, however, call for any changes in party rules or basic procedures. Even before the Republican convention they asked their delegates to watch Republican behavior and to be guided accordingly. And during the convention they watched the Republican proceedings carefully, in order to profit from any mistakes.[30]

The Democratic convention management took immediate steps to remedy the chief omission of the Republicans in physical arrangements: a good camera position to cover the speaker's rostrum head-on. A camera tower was placed on the floor about sixty feet in front of the platform, thus affording an excellent close-up view and avoiding distortion of the speaker and the confused and distracting background provided by the shirt-sleeve working press in the Republican convention. (Republican specialists have pointed out, however, that the installation of several teleprompters provided almost as much confusion for the Democratic speakers; with-

[30] *Broadcasting-Telecasting* (July 14, 1952), p. 6.

out coaching and experience, they were not sure which one to watch, or how to gauge their pace.) The Democrats eliminated the obviousness of the teleprompter, and the networks apparently were kind enough not to shoot pictures over the speaker's shoulder showing this device, as they had done in the Republican convention. The Democratic show thus lost such human interest as was offered by an impatient former President urging the teleprompter on.

The Democrats were not overtly divided into pro- and anti-television factions. They capitalized on the medium and took pains to address the television audience directly. They told the viewers that this was *their* convention, in an effort to enhance the Democratic line that theirs is the party of the people. Some party suggestions even transcended the bounds set by the television people, who counselled against supplementing speeches by special visual aids, on the ground that the best television tactics are to play the event straight. Party managers gave each network a complete "shooting script" each day in advance (it frequently could not be followed) and efforts were made to rehearse and time speakers and performers to match the scripts.

Chairman Frank McKinney, in short, promised a convention "tailored to TV." Other prominent Democrats, such as Senator Benton, predicted that television would revolutionize the conventions.[31] Chairman Rayburn disciplined parading delegates, asking them to keep their balloons from obstructing the television view of the speaker. Democratic monitors checked the television picture constantly, advising the management promptly if anything seemed to be going wrong. The Democrats took good care in dressing the convention hall to locate slogans and banners within convenient camera-shot. Thus key slogans would be transmitted country-wide and clearly associated with Democratic personalities and the

[31] The same (July 21, 1952), pp. 25 ff.

working of the party. The Democrats also exhorted their delegates, in the official convention program, in posters at headquarters, and in special leaflets placed on the chairs of the delegates, to be on time and to behave. The leaflets warned each delegate that he might provide a television close-up at any time.[32]

The Democratic delegates were on the whole more restrained than their Republican counterparts, and the convention itself a little more peaceful because of the prohibition against paid demonstrators. Despite thoughtful preparations, however, the Democrats were unable to shorten the speeches, get started on time, keep to schedule, or give a disciplined appearance to proceedings.

The first day of the Democratic convention was one of great interest and stress for the Democrats. There was Adlai Stevenson's welcome; an undercurrent of tension was building up all that day as the loyalty fight developed, and from midnight on, there was a furor about the Moody resolution. However important these events were to the politicians, television specialists thought that the convention got off to a "lackluster start."[33] The Democratic National Committee welcomed radio and television at its proceedings, but

[32] *Editor and Publisher* (July 26, 1952), pp. 9, 60. The text of one flyer distributed to Democratic delegates before the Republican convention read in part:

"It is likely that you and most of the rest of us participating in the Chicago convention will, at that time, make our first appearance as actors in a television production. We cannot rehearse our roles. We cannot always consciously govern our actions in light of the fact that whatever we do is being viewed by a substantial part of the population of America. But there are a few important things we can guard against in advance. For example, we can be in our seats well ahead of time . . . . We hope you will co-operate with us and see that your seat is always occupied when the Convention is officially in session.

"Another thing, it might be most helpful and instructive to observe how the Republican delegates behave (or misbehave). If you have television available to you, I suggest that you watch them with this in mind."

The flyer ended: "EVERY SEAT OCCUPIED—ON TIME—EVERY SESSION."

[33] See, for example, Jane Pinkerton in *Broadcasting-Telecasting* (July 28, 1952), pp. 23, 32 ff.

they were only sporadically covered, since with one exception they were not particularly controversial or dramatic. But the exception was a real one: the Moody-Roosevelt drive for loyalty affirmations. Despite statements that all Democratic proceedings would be open to all media, some of the delegation caucuses were understandably enough held in private. This opened the way to a major scoop of the convention: Martin Agronsky of ABC brought a camera to bear on the Louisiana caucus discussing the proposed loyalty amendment. He found an obscure opening into the caucus room, and although unable to pick up the debate, accompanied his video signal by a running account of what he thought the delegates were saying.[34]

Controversy and action on the floor were at a low ebb during the second and third days—a period the networks found hard to fill with lively material. The real action was going on in the convention committees and in delegate caucuses.[35] Tuesday on the floor was devoted to a "ladies day" program, with speeches by Perle Mesta, Eugenie Anderson, Georgia Neese Clark, India Edwards, and Eleanor Roosevelt. Wednesday's proceedings picked up a bit as the first barrages were fired in the loyalty fight on the floor. Senator Kefauver's entry on the floor, violating an unwritten rule of long standing, gave a fillip to events with a twenty-five-minute demonstration. The evening session returned to oratory and demonstrations. Not until after midnight did the convention (and parts of the country) see Rayburn put off Kefauver's minority report on the platform until after adoption, and then restrict him to one minute's discussion with no chance of a vote.[36] This relative ebb was ended by the Thursday session, in which fourteen hours ostensibly devoted to nominating

[34] The same, p. 34.
[35] See Paul T. David, Malcolm Moos, Ralph M. Goldman, *Presidential Nominating Politics in 1952*, Vol. I (1954), pp. 127–28.
[36] The same, pp. 135–36.

speeches were consumed with the seating of the Virginia, South Carolina, and Louisiana delegations.

As the conventions went on, the networks adjusted their tactics and procedures. Television portable equipment did not prove satisfactory, giving at best a murky picture. In the Republican convention the networks found it preferable to cover floor events by combining a radio signal from walkie-talkies carried by roving reporters on the floor with video provided by long-range lens cameras from the booths. Such reporters could follow meetings on the floor, interview personalities, and make commentary on the spot. The Republicans in particular objected to such activities; from time to time they would close the floor to radio-television reporters, who exercised their customary reportorial ingenuity to circumvent the bans, often with some success. But the vigorous and largely successful effort to keep portable radio and television equipment off the floor was doubtless of some value in preventing further breakdown in the decorum of the proceedings. Walkie-talkies and their bearers were a visibly disrupting influence wherever they appeared on the floor— although perhaps not much more so than certain types of interviewing on the floor by the pencil-and-paper reporters, who were usually permitted to roam about freely.

During the Democratic convention, the networks relied less on the pool coverage, and more on remote pickups, sending their reporters to the committee, delegation, and candidate headquarters in search of news, features, and scoops. Newsmen also concentrated on "home interest" material; the networks cut down on studio commentary, and increased shots of floor occurrences and personalities. Delegates capitalized on these efforts, crowding around the interview groups on the floor, making faces, waving banners, hands, and hats and shoving for preferred positions.

Film coverage was more prominent in the Democratic convention, especially by NBC, which developed a "hot process" for fast development of news film for showing. Film was shown by several local stations, all networks, and allied interests, including the Hearst newsreel chain. Under the most favorable conditions, film could be shown within a half-hour of shooting. News clips with strictly local significance were filmed and air-mailed to the appropriate local stations for showing.

Despite this latter emphasis on commentary, local interest, and peripheral events, television coverage in 1952 stressed the central story of the convention more than in 1948. In the earlier year the network directors were more concerned with demonstrating the novel capabilities of the medium; with four years' experience they were better prepared to deal with the convention on a more mature level. The networks considered that their main job was to tell the story of the convention itself—how the political party went about seating its delegates, adopting its platform, and selecting its candidates. Only when these basic procedures appeared to the broadcasters to be slow, inaccessible, or dull, did the networks, under some pressure of public complaints, divert attention from the main thread of events.

Total time devoted by the networks to covering the Democratic convention was somewhat greater than that devoted to the Republican convention. The actual time that the Republi-

Network	Hours of Coverage[37]	
	Republican	Democratic
CBS..........................	68	71
NBC..........................	75	77
ABC..........................	70	75
Total.....................	213	223
Average...................	71	74h 20 m.

can convention was in session was not as great as that for the Democratic. The former took 38 hours, 23 minutes, and the

[37] Source: *Broadcasting-Telecasting* (July 14, 21 and Aug. 4, 1952).

latter 45 hours, 52 minutes. Thus the networks gave some 32 hours more time to the Republican and 29 hours more to the Democratic convention than the actual duration of each formal event. The additional coverage can be roughly divided as follows: major attention was given on the opening morning of both conventions to commentary and human interest coverage of personalities. On the second and third days of the Republican convention, the networks devoted most of their attention prior to the assembling of the convention itself to the meetings of the credentials committee. Similarly, a good deal of time was devoted on the morning of the second day of the Democratic National Convention to the work of the credentials committee. The remainder of the time recorded by the networks as convention broadcasting that did not occur within the gavel-to-gavel time periods was devoted to commentary, interviews, coverage of the delegation and committee headquarters, and the production of special shows.

During the periods of each day while the conventions were in formal session, the great bulk of television time was spent in reporting events within the convention halls, according to logs maintained at the time under the auspices of the American Political Science Association.[38] Proportion-

[38] Logs of both the Republican and Democratic convention television coverage were prepared by two monitors—Edward Sherman and Howard Taslitz—in Chicago at the headquarters of the Cooperative Research Project on Convention Delegations. The monitors had available only a single television receiver and the reception conditions were difficult in the downtown office building at 19 S. LaSalle Street where the project office was located. The monitors estimated that 60 per cent of their coverage came from ABC, 30 per cent from CBS, and the remaining 10 per cent from NBC. The NBC signal was available only intermittently, and the Dumont signal was not available to loggers at all. The loggers estimated that ABC offered less commentary and interpretive news than CBS but more of the convention itself, and was giving fuller coverage of the subsidiary events surrounding the activities on the convention floor. Therefore their reports would tend to overstress those elements in which ABC was strong. The logs were intended to start with each formal session and continue until a formal recess. Actually the loggers provided additional monitoring on those days in which procedures closely related to the convention—i.e., the convention committee meetings—were in progress. But their total coverage is considerably less than that reported by each network as its total for the two conventions. The loggers inspected 50 hours, 35 minutes of Republican coverage, and 55 hours, 35 minutes of Democratic coverage.

ately, the networks paid more attention to floor proceedings at the Democratic than at the Republican conventions. Of the 45 hours and 52 minutes total Democratic convention time (exclusive of within-session recesses), the logs show all but 5 hours and 11 minutes with the picture coming from the hall. The Republican proceedings at the hall were carried all but 6 hours and 37 minutes out of a total of 38 hours and 29 minutes of gavel-to-gavel time. In each convention, there was one instance in which the networks spent a large portion of time away from the hall. On Wednesday afternoon, July 9, ABC and CBS spent most of their time with the Republican credentials committee rather than with floor events: 2 hours and 16 minutes out of a total of 3 hours and 45 minutes for the first session on that day. And on Thursday, July 24, during nearly 14 hours that were spent on nomination speeches and the seating of the critical delegations, ABC spent 2 hours and 10 minutes outside the hall: 20 minutes on interviews, 66 minutes on studio commentary and interviews, and 44 minutes on station breaks and advertising. Disregarding these two abnormal days, it can be seen that these networks spent the overwhelming proportion of their time in the convention hall itself while formal sessions were going on. There are no consolidated records showing what the other networks were doing on these occasions.

Some idea of the variety of advertising interlarded into convention coverage is provided by the APSA log. The Chicago stations not only spent time in mentioning the products of Westinghouse, Admiral, and Philco; there was mention of Armour hams, Lifesavers, Royal typewriters, Fox Deluxe and Stag beer, Bulova watches, Balaban and Katz movies, Swift products, SOS cleaner, Rival and Ideal dog food, Electrolux cleaners, United Airlines, Land-O-Lakes butter, Breeze detergent, Sunkist citrus products, Dunhill cigarettes, Borden milk products, and others.

The time logs confirm the general observation that as the conventions wore on, the frequency and length of advertising spots increased, especially on Thursday and Friday in the Democratic convention. The networks used more floor interviews with personalities in the hall during proceedings, thus reducing attention to the story itself as it slowly developed. Given the time requirements and the complexity of the Democratic voting arrangements, this development is not surprising.

Coverage of the minor party conventions was far more restricted. These were treated more as news than as special events up to the point of the acceptance speeches. The Progressive party, in a vigorous letter to the Federal Communications Commission, demanded equal convention coverage. But the FCC reply[39] made clear that access by a *party* to television was governed on the basis of fairness and general interest in the presentation of public events, not by the requirement of Section 315 that candidates shall have equal access. The letter also said that any broadcast licensee "who has made or proposes to make opportunities available for acceptance speeches by one candidate for a particular office is under a firm obligation to make equal opportunities available to all other legally qualified candidates for that office." Read out to 1,700 Progressive delegates assembled in Chicago, it was acclaimed as a great victory.[40]

Nevertheless, the Progressive Party Convention was poorly covered by all media, despite its unusual features and the place of the party in the political spectrum.[41] Its candidate, Vincent Hallinan, could not attend because he was

[39] Letter, FCC to the Progressive party, dated July 2, 1952, released July 7, 1952, FCC file number FCC-52-649 77135.

[40] *Editor and Publisher* (July 12, 1952), p. 13.

[41] The same, and *The Nation* (July 12, 1952), which pointed out editorially the almost complete blackout of news coverage, and lamented this lack of attention to a "significant source of criticism from the Left."

serving a sentence for contempt of court. His wife delivered his acceptance speech, which CBS recorded and rebroadcast by radio after the convention. NBC worked a film summary of this convention into a broadcast preceding the Republican convention, and ABC gave it fifteen minutes of time on both television and radio on July 5.[42]

The letter of the Progressive party and the FCC reply emphasized that once a candidate is nominated, he is no longer the candidate for the nomination of a party but is a nominee for government office, and as such he is entitled to opportunity to use broadcast media equal to that offered any other presidential nominee. The various networks carried, on sustaining time, the acceptance speeches of candidates of the lesser parties, including the Socialist Labor party, the Socialist party, the Socialist Workers party, the American Vegetarian party, and the Prohibition party, as well as the Progressive party.

The Immediate Response

The evidence of actual viewer reaction to television presentation of the conventions is scanty and scattered. The simpler questions are: How many people were in the television audience, and where were they? The more pertinent additional questions are: What did they think about what they saw, and what did they do about it? There is considerable evidence bearing on the first two questions, most of it provided by market research agencies. There is little evidence about the latter two, since the public opinion polls and surveys paid more attention to the role of television in the post-convention period. Some additional evidence that bears on these latter points appears in letters to editors, telephone calls to networks, to sponsors, or to the party committees, or in communications to the convention management contempo-

[42] *Broadcasting-Telecasting* (July 14, 1952), p. 32.

raneous with the convention itself—all largely inaccessible or gone today.

Taking the simpler questions first, it appears that very sizable audiences looked at both conventions. The A. C. Nielsen Company[43] reported a total of 185,500,000 home-hours of listening to the Republican convention, a Democratic total of 257,500,000. The peak number of different homes tuned in during any one day of the Republican convention was 13,097,000 compared to a peak total of 14,556,000 homes tuned in to the Democratic convention. The conventions drew better daytime audiences than "normal" daytime television, but did not approach in popularity the most popular evening entertainment shows.

Nationwide statistics on the balance of viewing were not paralleled in all areas. The Pulse index, based on a sample of 12,500 households in the greater New York metropolitan area, showed that more people saw the Republican convention; it had an average rating of 43.0 at night, and 16.5 in the afternoon. The Democratic convention was rated at 32.0 at night, and 12.2 in the afternoon. A day-by-day check of evening listening showed the Republican convention with more viewers than the Democratic except on the Friday of each convention.[44]

Nielsen plotted profiles of nationwide convention viewing that show by half-hour intervals the number of homes tuned to the conventions on television, and compared these profiles with those of normal viewing in preceding weeks.[45] The pattern of convention viewing was consistently heavier than in the preceding normal week, except for the peak hours

[43] Special tabulation prepared by A. C. Nielsen Company, and press releases of Aug. 12 and Sept. 8, 1952.

[44] *Broadcasting-Telecasting* (Aug. 4, 1952), p. 32. The Pulse figures represent sets in use in television homes; a rating of 43.0 means that 43 sets out of 100 are tuned to a particular program during the critical time interval of the survey.

[45] The convention profiles accompanied Nielsen press releases of Aug. 12 and Sept. 8, 1952. The comparison of convention viewing with viewing in the preceding week was furnished to clients privately in 1952.

of evening listening (from 9 to 11 P.M.). The audience gain was most marked during the afternoon.

These profiles give some basis for concluding that the amount of viewing is roughly related to variations in the importance of and interest in the particular occurrences of each convention. In the Republican convention, extensive viewing coincided with the MacArthur keynote speech, the Hoover speech, the Dirksen speech on seating the Georgia delegation, and with the nomination speeches on Thursday night, July 10. Top viewing occurred during the speeches nominating Senator Taft, between 10:30 and 11:00 P.M. EDST, when 8,655,000 homes were looking at the convention. The Eisenhower nomination speech came very late, starting at 12:40 A.M. EDST; even at this hour an audience of 4,477,000 homes was watching. The low audience for the Republican convention came on Tuesday between 3:30 and 4:00 P.M. EDST, when 881,000 homes were viewing the credentials committee proceedings while the convention was in recess.[46] Morning viewing had been substantial, with a total of 4,160,000 homes tuned in to see the credentials committee, then considering the Florida delegation.

Wednesday morning over 3,500,000 homes were tuned in, but during the afternoon the audience dwindled to a low of 1,550,000 homes between 4:00 and 4:30 P.M. EDST, as the credentials committee continued its work on seating the Texas delegation. After 5:00 P.M., as it concluded, 2,626,000 homes were watching. It was on this afternoon that Senator McCarthy made his major speech to the convention, using such audio-visual aids as red-herring placards labeled Hiss, Lattimore, and Acheson. Even with these histrionics, Mc-

[46] As used in this analysis, the general rubric "convention" covers the whole event, including committee meetings, caucuses of state delegations, and similar related activities. The lowest point of viewing in the entire Republican convention week came between 6:30 and 7:00 P.M. on Monday as plotted by Nielsen. The number of homes had slumped to 864,000 from a figure of 4,548,000 in the preceding half-hour. At this low point, the convention had recessed and no related event was being covered live.

Carthy could not assemble an outstanding audience or retain what he had; viewers dropped from 2,626,000 in the half hour when he commenced his address, to 1,551,000 in the next half hour. The credentials committee meeting a half-hour later (after the convention had recessed) was enjoying an audience as good as the one with which McCarthy started.

The Democratic peak audience of 10,161,000 homes was reached during the half hour from 10:30 to 11:00 P.M. EDST on Friday, July 25, during the third ballot which led to the Stevenson nomination. At the time of the nomination itself—the end of the ballot, 1:31 A.M. EDST—an audience of 6,774,000 homes was watching. Other points of peak listening in the Democratic convention came during the Rayburn and Barkley speeches on Wednesday evening (7,283,000 homes and 5,859,000 homes respectively); during the period from 9:00 to 11:00 P.M. EDST on Thursday when the question of seating the Virginia delegation was being decided (7,719,000 to 8,487,000 homes); and during the balloting on the afternoon of Friday, July 25 (7,258,000 homes). The low point in the Democratic convention came between 4:30 and 5:00 P.M. EDST, on Tuesday, July 22, during the credentials committee meeting considering the case of Mississippi (1,270,000 homes).

Although the Democratic convention was adjudged dull by some commentators for the first three days, it is significant that at no time did its audience drop as low as the Republican audience at its lowest, and that the peak audience during this period was a very substantial one—over 7,200,000 homes during the Rayburn speech.

One factor maintaining the audience was that none of the important network programs was available to the local stations during the period of the conventions. All were pre-empted. While local stations were theoretically free to originate shows of their own, we have no evidence that they did; and it would have been hazardous for them to try, since the conventions might at any time have offered a striking news development. What they could do, and undoubtedly did to a considerable extent, was to interpolate film clips made to appeal to local audiences—actions of local people and occurrences of special local or regional significance.

An important development in citizen participation in the electoral process brought about first by radio, and later by television, is the opportunity for members or adherents of one party to look in on the proceedings of their opponents. It is a cliché of political commentary that political rallies are rarely attended by adherents of the opposing party, and then usually for heckling or for information; hence the opportunities for conversion are small. But with radio, the chance to tune in requires little physical effort and far less personal involvement than would actual attendance at an opposing party function. Television matched radio's ease of admission, and added the dimension of sight to sound—a factor increasing the viewer's sense of participation. The various studies of convention watching do not specify the degree to which viewers observed opposing party proceedings, but the over-all figures for political viewing make the conclusion almost certain that there was a great deal of this overlapping. (The Miami study discussed below does indicate the extent to which Democratic members of its panel viewed Republican campaign speeches, and vice versa.)

Granted that there was a wide audience for the conventions, what do we know about the impact of this event on the viewers? There is little in the way of carefully analyzed data that would support conclusions valid for the nation as a whole. Some light is thrown on the impact of the conventions on viewers by an unpublished study made for NBC shortly after each convention of the responses of sample audiences in New York. These findings are at best only suggestive, even for the New York area, but they do indicate, with

somewhat greater precision than would narrative accounts
of variously placed observers (or expressions of personal
opinion or bias), what was the range of television impact and
its direction in a metropolitan area in 1952. This study examined, by pre-convention and post-convention interviewing,
the responses of 310 viewers of the Republican and 341
viewers of the Democratic convention. It explored interest
in voting, previous voting experience, plans for voting in
the next presidential election, and knowledge of the candidates and convention methods. It asked about sources of convention news and evaluation of the source or sources providing most complete information. It examined the role of television as a news medium, the degree of viewing, and the
respondent's evaluation of television coverage. The dates of
the two interviews were from June 30 to July 6 for the pre-
convention test; from July 28 to August 4, 1952 for the post-
convention test.

It appeared that the conventions enlarged interest in voting
both in amount and degree, and increased preference for the
Republican party. Viewing intensified interest in the conventions, and increased reliance on television as a main
source of information about the conventions and elections at
the expense of magazines, radio, conversation, and newspapers, in that order.[47] Viewing did not greatly augment the
awareness of the current position of the various candidates,
since this was high to begin with, but it did increase notably
the amount of respondents' information about who the

[47] The Republican viewer panel rated the sources of information as follows:

Main Source of News	Pre-Convention (Per cent)	Post-Convention (Per cent)	Change (Per cent)
TV	39.8	49.8	+10.0
Newspapers	33.9	33.4	− 0.5
Radio	16.4	14.1	− 2.3
Magazines	8.3	2.0	− 6.3
Conversation	1.6	0.7	− 0.9
	100.0	100.0	

candidates were. Television was rated after the newspapers as the most important source in helping the respondents make up their minds. Except in the case of Kefauver, whose supporters rated television first, the supporters of the other candidates rated newspapers first and television second from this standpoint. Radio, magazines, and other sources followed in that order.

Television viewing increased information among viewers about the location, the composition, and procedure of the conventions, but most notably did not increase markedly the number who knew such technical items of information as the number of delegates it took to win the nomination in each convention. Respondents' scores after viewing moved toward the right answer, but those who actually made the right choice on this question were a surprisingly small number in view of the fact that the median number of hours watched was 10.4 per viewer, and the average 11.9 hours, and the further fact that the exercise of voting and the themes of the commentators turned so often on the achievement of the magic number needed for victory.

The respondents' estimates of the amount they learned seemed to run far ahead of their real increase in learning as judged by improved ability to answer technical questions about the organization and procedure of the conventions. Respondents' replies to the question: "What did you learn from watching the convention?" were distributed as follows among the following categories:

	Per cent
Workings and procedure	39.3
Politics, politicians	15.8
Confusion, lack of dignity	13.4
Candidates and their policies	11.3
Republican party policies	10.1
People should be responsible (national primary)	6.1
TV can bring you closer	3.2
Miscellaneous	4.9
Nothing learned	18.2

Respondents made a great variety of statements, which formed the basis for the foregoing classification. These statements, taken in their raw form, indicate a surprising range of comment and some odd contradictions. Respondents said, among other things, concerning the Republican convention:

You can't beat machine politicians.
Conniving doesn't pay.
Taft was pushed aside because of politics.
Conventions should give more attention to prominent speakers, make less noise.
Disgusted with politics, and their "carnival attitude."
The democratic process at work. Old guard politicians are really not wanted.
Republicans are a bad lot.
Republican leadership is nominal, not representative.
I met a lot of loathsome politicians who are completely insincere.
Learned a lot about procedure. [This response recurred frequently.]
Learned that delegates can change votes anytime during the convention.
Learned a lot about the workings of politics you could never get from the newspapers.
Learned never to attend one. Should cut the conventions out to save money.

Similar comments were made on the Democratic convention a few weeks later.

The analysis of respondents' replies to questions asked prior to and after the Democratic convention revealed information paralleling in a general way the results gained from interviewing the panel of Republican convention viewers. Television seemed less effective in increasing interest in the conventions among the second group of respondents. But viewing the Democratic convention on television not only increased the viewers' preference for the Democratic candidates but also increased the preference for the Republican candidates even more. These increases were shifts from previous responses favoring independent candidates, and from "don't know" pre-convention responses.[48] Thus television seems to have helped voters crystallize their judgment in favor of the stronger candidates.

Among the second panel, the gain of television as a main source of news and information about conventions and elections was considerably greater than among the earlier panel; news and magazines lost far more sharply than radio or conversation as a news source. The pattern of judgment as to which medium was most helpful in making up the voters' minds remained the same, however; news led television in every group except that which preferred Kefauver. Television was given the lead, far and away ahead of any of its competitors, as having done the "best job of coverage."

This study was conducted in the city where television has its longest history; the sample is very small, and unrepresentative of the nation either from a geographical or demographic point of view.

The public opinion polls did not report much of significance. Elmo Roper confined himself to the question of how well the candidates handled themselves; he discovered that the best-liked Republican was Hoover, the best-liked Democrat was Rayburn, and that Dewey and Dirksen scored high in both the like and dislike columns. The imputed reason for this apparent anomaly was that both Dewey and Dirksen were important in *intra*-party encounters.[49]

The press included such items as Earl Godwin's report

---

[48] The preference figures are as follows:

Party Preference	Pre-Convention (Per cent)	Post-Convention (Per cent)
Republican	33.1	37.8
Democratic	26.4	29.9
Independent	4.4	2.1
Don't know	36.1	30.2
	100.0	100.0

[49] *New York Herald Tribune* (Aug. 11, 1952).

(after the Republican convention) that every delegate he had interviewed on one morning had called long distance to friends or relatives to find out from them—as television viewers—what was happening, since the out-of-town viewers had a better concept of the convention than the delegates.[50] The radio-television trade press claimed that their media "put Eisenhower over": he was able, via these media, to offset four years of Taft plans, organization, and operations. Taft forces charged that 90 per cent of the commentators and reporters favored Eisenhower; a charge hotly denied by broadcasters and their spokesmen who pointed out, however, that the Taft organization was hard to get along with during the convention, whereas the Eisenhower staff co-operated all down the line.[51]

Television's claim to have "put Ike over" should be evaluated in the light of such findings as those of Herbert Hyman and Paul Sheatsley, who analyzed 1947 and 1948 data to show Eisenhower's enormous political strength even at that early date.[52] These authors drew the conclusion that personality had more effect upon the outcome in 1952 than issues of Communism, corruption, and Korea. They did not commit themselves on the influence of media in producing this outcome.

Popular and press opinion was considerably scattered, following, for the most part, the established preferences of the observers. One instance of shock is provided by Douglas

[50] *Broadcasting-Telecasting* (July 14, 1952), p. 26.
[51] The same, p. 102.
[52] Herbert Hyman and Paul Sheatsley, "The Political Appeal of President Eisenhower," *Public Opinion Quarterly* (Winter 1953–54), pp. 443–60. The authors point out that Eisenhower was the most frequent spontaneous voters' choice for President in a National Opinion Research Center Poll in three states in May 1948; he outran Truman in a September 1947 Gallup Poll. He was consistently the first choice of independent voters; was strongly endorsed by leaders of both parties. All this strength was mustered despite the facts that (a) his party preference was unknown; (b) he made no statements of position on outstanding current issues, and (c) he strongly stressed that he was not available for nomination.

Foster's article, "Window on the Smoke-Filled Room"[53] in which he concluded that the conventions were no more than camouflages of the political machines at work, a vast marionette show, a "fatuous exhibition of phoniness" that raised doubts about the reality of American democracy.

Although there is little direct evidence of the immediate reaction of the commercial sponsors, they had good cause to be pleased. They got more hours than they bargained for or initially expected. They completely disposed of some lines of goods, and got a huge if not selected audience for references to or demonstrations of the remainder. While the audience measurement services did not place the conventions on a par with "I Love Lucy," the sponsors nevertheless secured solid, nationwide attention for their products over a protracted period of time.[54]

The first reaction of the networks after the closing of the conventions and the return of equipment to headquarters was an enormous sigh. Publicly the networks congratulated themselves on public service, on demonstration of the value of the medium of television in the competition for the ad-

[53] *The Nation* (Aug. 16, 1952), p. 131.

[54] See, for example, the article, "Philco Still Counting the Chips from $3,000,000 Political Gamble," in *Advertising Age* (Nov. 17, 1952), pp. 44–45. Although this article summarizes the effects of the total program of convention and election coverage, it seems apparent that the convention coverage played a vital part. Philco introduced a new multi-wave radio set during the conventions. Although several months were expected to elapse before sales would develop markedly, distributors and dealers had to put customers on allocation within weeks of the debut. Air-conditioning commercials were withdrawn during the Democratic convention because orders had already become too heavy to handle. Philco increased strictly institutional commercials to be sandwiched in with selling commercials during the election returns sponsorship. John Gilligan, vice president and advertising director, said that: "We consider this promotion one of the most successful things we have undertaken. It has been almost unbelievably successful from an advertising standpoint, from a public relations standpoint, and from a sales standpoint."

The commercials were started during the pre-convention period, as the politicians gathered. Philco began getting letters and postcards on their commercials immediately. Some 15,000 letters were received, of which the company judged 90 per cent to approve the mixed live and filmed commercials. A critical 10 per cent objected mostly for political reasons or because they did not like the commentators.

vertiser's dollar, and made discreet references to their net financial losses from convention television.[55] The sheer physical effort of the broadcasting personnel and the engineers was prodigious. But much like the Yankee brigade in the Civil War, of which it was said after its first engagement that it was always thereafter ready for battle but never again eager, the men of the networks never dreamed that they would not cover conventions in the future.They were soon considering afresh the special problems of convention coverage in the light of the recent experience and that of the ongoing campaign.

Some television newsmen questioned the value of the conventions themselves. Much of the convention experience was adjudged dull, but television officials and newsmen felt that the medium should record and communicate what happens. And the preponderance of immediate sentiment among the industry men was that there should be more factuality rather than less in reporting the event. *Fortune* quoted William McAndrew, who emerged from the convention experience as NBC's chief of news for both radio and television, as suggesting that the 1952 experience might mark the end of the conventions as such and lead to a national primary.[56] *Fortune's* reporter took a different point of view:

[55] Because of the joint nature of these deals it is impossible to say how much it cost the networks to cover the conventions by television alone. *Fortune* estimated that they stood to lose about $2 million on political coverage in 1952 as a whole. The highest estimates of the gross cost of carrying the conventions and election, including cost of pre-empting established programs, ran about $10 million. Westinghouse paid CBS $3 million; Admiral paid ABC $2 million; and NBC said Philco paid them $2.75 million for complete election coverage. (*Fortune*, September 1952, pp. 86, 210.) The writer was told by an NBC official in September 1954, that the *Fortune* figures were about as close as the networks could estimate. Frank Stanton of CBS later testified that while Columbia did not make anything on the election coverage as a whole, it didn't lose much either. Losses of the other networks were put at the order of several million. But the networks said the money had been well spent, not only as a public service, but also because of the phenomenal sale of television sets, which immediately heightened the influence and later the time rates of television as a medium of communication and of advertising.

[56] *Fortune* (September 1952), p. 210.

But conventions have been going on many more years than TV, and politicians have been around even longer than that. It is more likely that TV will end up by trimming itself. The determination to record each of the Chicago affairs down to its last tiresome detail, and with a minimum of interpretative comment, was due in a measure to TV's lack of editorial experience and lack of editorial nerve. The fact of the matter is, the industry is already pondering how to cover the 1956 conventions with a maximum effect of excitement and interest.[57]

[57] The same.

CHAPTER III

Further Evolution

DEVELOPMENTS in television during the campaign of 1952, the assessment of impact of television on politics, the growth and development of television as a communications medium from 1952 to the present, and the experience in the off-year 1954 races have all contributed to current estimates of the role of television in the presidential nominating process in 1956 and future years.

The Campaign of 1952

With the conclusion of television coverage of the Democratic National Convention, developments in the relationship of television to politics came to a brief halt. Immediately after the conventions, the visible portions of the political campaign went into a comparative lull, and political television with them. There was little of it during August, as both candidates deferred their barnstorming and television appearances until the traditional campaign opening on Labor Day. (Both had made important foreign policy speeches to the American Legion in August.) But there was plenty of action behind the scenes. The Republicans had a change of television command, with Robert Humphreys succeeding William Mylander. The Republicans chose their advertising agencies (Kudner and Batten, Barton, Durstine & Osborn), "blueprinted" their campaign, and deployed their forces in preparation for the forthcoming struggle. The Democrats proceeded with their television preparations without breaking stride, having already made many commitments that could not easily be changed by their newly chosen candidate or by the new national committee chairman, if, indeed, there was any disposition to make important changes.

The television strategy of the parties appears in retrospect, at least, to have differed in important ways.[1] The Republicans estimated that they did not need to put their candidate through an extensive course of nationwide television appearances, since his face was already widely known to the American people, and his public personality had been well and favorably projected by news media for a decade. The Republicans discovered that Eisenhower's appearances at the convention had generated fresh interest in him as a person. His pledge to visit every nook and cranny of the country loosed a spate of requests for public appearances. The party wanted to demonstrate his grassroots appeal and to stress regional interests and policies. For such a campaign, regional television and radio would be most suitable. And there was at least a relative shortage of Republican cash, in view of the planned policy of pre-empting shows and buying more extensive station arrays than their opponents. All these reasons, plus the feeling that the party needed special efforts to heal rifts, underlay a decision to send Eisenhower whistle-stopping instead of concentrating on nationwide network television and radio.

The Democrats, however, needed to make Stevenson into a well-known national figure, to advertise his policies and his positions, and to answer Republican arguments and attacks that would develop during the course of the campaign. The Democrats were also interested in making special impact on minority and foreign-language groups.

A study made at Miami University (Ohio) indicates that the pattern of limited television provided by the parties was

[1] See the summary report, "What Air Media Did to Swing the Vote," in *Sponsor* (Nov. 3, 1952), pp. 25–27, 89–94, which briefs the strategy and operations of both parties in the use of radio and television.

more than matched by a pattern of light television viewing. During the summer, entertainment was preferred to politics on television, and the pattern of limited viewing was continued beyond September, until within a few days of the election itself.[2]

A main exception to the rule of light post-convention political viewing was the Nixon explanation of his financial affairs on September 23, an event that would qualify as of special public interest even apart from its political status. According to the Nielsen Television Index, this was far and away the most looked-at event during the active campaign. It was carried by NBC over an array of 62 stations and was seen in an estimated total of 9,136,000 homes, commanding 48.9 per cent of the available television audience. CBS also carried the Nixon telecast.

Not until election eve did the audiences approach this figure. Both parties brought their campaigns to a climax with television over three networks. Stevenson, appearing over 89 stations and reaching into 7,500,000 homes, achieved the largest audience of the campaign between 10:30 and 11:00 P.M. EDST. During the ensuing hour, the Republicans "reported" to Eisenhower and Nixon in a program carried by 83 stations and reaching 7,300,000 homes, via three networks. This night was the only occasion during the campaign when either of the parties bought simultaneous time over more than one network. Eisenhower had been on both ABC and NBC (50 stations) earlier in the evening, reaching into 6,232,000

[2] Department of Marketing, Miami University, *The Influence of Television on the 1952 Elections* (1954), p. 36. Cited below as the Miami study. This study reported that only 5.1 per cent of their panel reported viewing the Stevenson Labor Day speech, and only 10.6 per cent saw Eisenhower's Philadelphia speech the following Thursday (September 4). Only 7.6 per cent heard Stevenson's foreign policy speech at San Francisco on the 9th. Seibert and his associates put the "turning point" marking a return to sizable viewing on October 24, when Eisenhower made his dramatic promise in Detroit to go to Korea. The members of the Department who participated in the study were Joseph C. Seibert, Chairman, and A. J. Alton, Hubert E. Bice, Lee S. McDonald, Robert H. Myers, and William F. Suhring.

homes. Otherwise the parties concentrated their operations in one network at a time.[3]

The next most popular campaign telecast was that of Nixon on October 29, reaching 6 million homes via CBS. Other notable performances included that of President Truman on October 22 (5,956,000 homes, via 55 stations) and Senator McCarthy on October 27 (5,002,000 homes via 48 stations). The Republican policy of buying more stations and pre-empting established programs seemed to pay off, as 11 Republican telecasts drew audiences of more than 5 million homes, while only three Democratic telecasts passed the 5 million figure. The low audience for the campaign was drawn by Eisenhower, when only 236,000 homes were tuned in for his quarter-hour over NBC on the afternoon of November 1, which was telecast by only 12 stations.

Relatively higher interest in the conventions over television seems indicated by the fact that at no one time during the campaign did any speech or event mass as many viewers as the peak of 10,161,000 homes reached during the Democratic convention, and only the Nixon apologia exceeded the Republican convention peak of 8,655,000 homes. On election night, however, there was a peak election returns audience of 11,971,000 homes tuned in between 10:00 and 10:30 P.M. EDST. This event was the first since the conventions to be carried by all networks, and there was no competition within the medium.

Although programs of both parties were usually timed so as not to compete with good shows, the factor of competition with other programs was important. In single-station

[3] The pattern of network use is interesting. Taking the Nielsen array of 1952 presidential telecasts, totaling 45, 22 were by Democrats, 22 by Republicans, and one by Wayne Morse (then a Republican senator supporting Stevenson). The Republicans consistently bought more stations; 15 of their broadcasts were on 50 stations or more, as compared to 6 Democratic broadcasts. Two Republican and 5 Democratic broadcasts were carried on from 40 to 50 stations. Five Republican and 11 Democratic broadcasts were on 39 stations or less. The minimum array used by either party was 11. Based on special tabulation by A. C. Nielsen Company, copyright 1953.

markets, the outlet might not decide to take the political show, thus cutting off any political viewers in its area.

During the campaign, the most notable development in the strategy of use of television and radio was the strong concentration on selective radio-television spot announcements, used most heavily by the Republicans in the closing weeks. These announcements were placed adjacent to the most popular shows and concentrated in those areas and attuned to those audiences that the Republican strategists thought were most important to securing victory. They were more interested in reaching the non-voter than the switch-voter. The Democrats used similar techniques, but far less extensively because of a smaller budget, and because they had already reserved substantial blocks of time for speeches and panels.[4] Both Democrats and Republicans worked within the established forms and procedures of the medium, with each scoring mild successes; the Clare Booth Luce documentary on September 30 was notable for the Republicans,[5] and the "Campaigning with Stevenson" documentary for the Democrats. The Stevenson documentary reached 2,700,000

[4] See "Saturation of Radio and TV Spots Seems to Have Paid Off for G.O.P.," *Advertising Age* (Nov. 10, 1952), p. 3. This article reports that Republicans spent between $1.3 and $1.5 million on the spot drive (Republican sources later estimated the total at about $800,000), of which some $275,000 was spent in the New York City area alone. There were over 120 spots per day shown there. The campaign was planned to saturate 11 states: New York, New Jersey, Illinois, Massachusetts, Michigan, Maryland, Indiana, California, Pennsylvania, Texas, and Connecticut. Heavy spot schedules were also run in Florida and Virginia. Ohio and Wisconsin came in for less attention, and in all, spots were run in 40 of the 48 states. The reported object was to cut into Democratic majorities in the cities, so the expected Republican strength in the suburbs and in rural areas could carry the day. The Democrats, it seems, planned a similar drive, chiefly in Ohio and in California (see Herbert R. Craig, "Distinctive Features of Radio-TV in the 1952 Presidential Campaign," unpublished Master's thesis, University of Iowa, 1954, p. 61). The Democrats blasted the Republican tactics, and demanded that the FCC take action on the ground that corporations were making bought time available to the Republican party, and thus making an illegal contribution. The FCC asked for further particulars, and took no action.

[5] This was carried over 57 stations and viewed by 3,128,000 homes. The Republican National Committee estimated the response as "tremendous," and repeated the formula on October 26. This show, adjudged less successful, was carried by 33 ABC stations, and reached 1,322,000 homes.

homes via a 48-station NBC network. For the most part, however, both parties relied on speeches of the candidates as the most important single type of television-radio usage.

Development in technique for the use of the television speech was notable, as illustrated by the Nixon explanation, which was called both masterpiece and soap opera by contemporary critics. On September 14, 1955, Nixon himself revealed that the broadcast was put off from Sunday until Tuesday night for two reasons, to give him time to prepare thoroughly and to build up the audience. "We wanted to create suspense." There was no rehearsal, because "when you rehearse you lose in spontaneity what you gain in smoothness." Mr. Nixon arrived at the studios only twenty minutes before the broadcast without a prompter or script other than five pages of notes.[6]

The Republicans spent some $3.5 million for radio-television campaigning, including some $2.1 million for network time. The Democrats spent about $2.5 million in all, and about $1.5 million on network time.[7] In contrast to the usual judgment that the Republicans had cash to spare to spend for campaign television, is the comment of a GOP spokesman reported by *Sponsor*[8] to the effect that financial contributions did not come in at the expected rate, as many contributors on whom the party had counted for gifts during the campaign said their contributions had already been made in order to get their candidate nominated, "And with the cost of TV the money we had just didn't stretch far enough. We had to trim down our plans for extensive TV coverage and depend largely on radio and the newspapers to spread the General's views on various matters."

There were several important problems of procedural

[6] "Nixon Tells How to Win TV Friends," *New York Times* (Sept. 15, 1955), p. 22.

[7] Craig, "Distinctive Features of Radio-TV in the 1952 Presidential Campaign," p. 125.

[8] *Sponsor* (Nov. 3, 1952), p. 90.

technique. The main one involved adjusting television appearances to the requirements of campaign travel, arranging matters so that major speeches would be made in cities that could *originate* network television, and that would be timed in accordance with the emerging requirements of the campaign, and adjusted to the political susceptibilities of the local and regional groups as well as the national television audience. Other problems involved planning for television time purchases. The Republicans made no advance commitments and had to decide whether to meet the additional costs of pre-empting prime time already occupied by established shows, or to take less desirable time at a lower figure. They chose the former course deliberately in order to win the additional audiences assumed to come from the habit of viewers of tuning in at the time of the most desirable shows. The Democrats had laid their plans in May before the convention; they decided to fit their requirements into prime time, but not on nights when popular and established shows were already fixtures. They reserved time well in advance in the hope they would have the money to pay for it according to the network's terms.[9] The Democrats placed their shows at 10:30 to 11:00 P.M. on Tuesdays and Thursdays from September 2 through election day.[10] They hoped to capitalize on the regularity of the hour by developing a habit of tuning in. Their total pre-emption bill for the campaign was $750, to assure time on election eve.

Evidence of Impact

There is little doubt today among industry circles, political practitioners generally, commentators and publicists, and

[9] NBC policy granted no options for political broadcasts; required cash payment not less than 48 hours in advance; and provided that no political order might be cancelled less than 30 days before time of broadcast without payment in full. 1952 NBC Political Broadcast Procedures, pp. 1–2.

[10] *Sponsor* (Nov. 3, 1952), p. 27.

the lay public at large, that television coverage of the 1952 conventions and the subsequent campaign had important political effects; that television played a considerable role; and that politics and campaigning of the future would be markedly affected by the advent and development of the new medium. The industry and its spokesmen promptly asserted that their claims for the efficacy of television in informing the public and motivating a large vote were borne out. *Sponsor* reported:

> It has been said of this campaign that 1952 marks the "transition" year—that this is the year that the airwaves were linked with the whistle-stop; that 1952 will be the year in which people saw their last campaign train. The all-out air efforts of both parties in the final stages of the battle indicate that this year will be a model for all future political campaigns, with candidates competing for votes via radio-TV.[11]

William S. Paley, CBS Board Chairman, in accepting an award from the Poor Richard Club of Philadelphia on January 17, 1953, opined that 1952 was the first campaign in which television was a "dominating factor," and "the degree to which it shaped the mind and behavior of the individual American voter, the electorate as a whole, and the candidates themselves, still remains to be fully comprehended." Television stirred the individual voter out of his apathy, Paley continued, and gave him a more direct and intimate sense of participation in the political life of the nation than he had ever enjoyed before. Television gave the voter a deeper understanding of the issues involved, enlarging his capacity to understand and analyze the issues, and increasing the objectivity with which he considered them. Television was "a contributing factor of enormous weight" in achieving a record voter turnout of 63 millions.

But, Paley went on, the potential of television had not really been exploited. It had only been *added* to traditional

11 The same, p. 92.

modes of campaigning, involving extensive travel, speech-writing, and speechmaking. By using television and other modern means of communication, the conventions could be placed later and the campaign shortened to seven weeks. This would restrict the period of "controlled hostility" said to characterize this febrile period in our national life with benefit to all, at home and abroad, and during the same period the political parties could make an adequate impact.[12]

But scholarly studies take a more cautious view. Scientifically valid evidence of the impact of television on the campaign is scarce, and what is available is restricted in scope and cautiously interpreted. The Miami study, cited above, made by Seibert and Associates in Ohio, arrived at a modest appraisal. The reports of studies by Campbell and his colleagues at the Survey Research Center are largely noncommittal on the influence of television.[13] And Simon and Stern concluded, after comparing voting statistics in counties of high and of low television density in Iowa in 1952, that there were no statistically reliable differences either in turnout or in preference for the Republican candidate.[14]

The Miami study reasoned from a measurement of the course of precipitation of political decision made by its panel members, which revealed that the victory for Eisenhower came early.[15] About 75 per cent of those on the

[12] William S. Paley, "Television and the Presidential Campaign," CBS pamphlet.

[13] See Angus Campbell, Gerald Gurin, and Warren E. Miller, "Television and the Election," in *Scientific American* (May 1953), pp. 47 ff. In the volume by Campbell and Associates, *The Voter Decides* (1954), pp. 31–33, no separate attention to television is given at all. Interpretations of the role of the mass media are founded on an assumption that they are the chief means whereby a party communicates with its relevant publics, and are restricted to a generalized description of the "vicarious" participation of voters in the campaign via these media. Campbell is interested in plotting the voting behavior of panel members against the degree of their exposure to one or more of four mass media: television, radio, newspapers, and magazines.

[14] Herbert A. Simon and Frederick Stern, "The Effect of Television Upon Voting Behavior in Iowa in the 1952 Presidential Election," *American Political Science Review*, Vol. 49, No. 2 (June 1955), pp. 470–78.

[15] Miami study, Chap. 5, "The Role of Television," pp. 35 ff.

Miami panel who voted for Eisenhower had made up their minds to do so by the end of the conventions. During the subsequent campaign Eisenhower got only about one quarter of the total votes finally cast for him. Stevenson had attained half his votes by the end of the conventions and secured the other half later in the campaign. Thus the benefits of television to Eisenhower, concluded the Miami associates, must have come early; those for Stevenson, later. Television could well have played an important part in shaping the pre-convention preference for Eisenhower, as 83.4 per cent of the panel had seen him on television—more, in fact, than owned sets. (But, reports the study, even more had seen Taft and Truman.) Eisenhower had made a good impression, better than that made by Taft, Truman, or Kefauver. The conventions gave greater opportunities to make impressions via television than did any subsequent speech or event during the campaign. Among Miami's panel, there was more viewing of the MacArthur speech (59.3 per cent) than of any other convention or post-convention political event during the whole campaign. The Hoover speech was seen by 52.1 per cent; the Eisenhower acceptance speech by 48.8 per cent. For the Democrats, Barkley amassed the largest audience with 53.2 per cent, followed by Mrs. Roosevelt (48.8 per cent), and Stevenson's acceptance speech (35.3 per cent). The Nixon financial explanation was seen by 43.8 per cent of the panel.

Briefly summarized, the Miami study concluded that Eisenhower won because of certain personal characteristics, his stand on foreign policy, and a feeling that there was a need for a change in administration.[16] Television was *not* of vital importance to the winning of Eisenhower votes by personality factors.[17] He gained more from newspapers. Steven-

[16] The same, p. 35.
[17] The same, p. 41. The judgment is based on gains in pro-Eisenhower opinion during the conventions, in which those who followed the conventions on television

son did gain more from television in terms of favorable appraisal of personality factors.[18]

The Miami group concluded that television possessed no characteristics superior to those of other media with respect to transmission of public understanding of political statements.[19] The study used as a standard of quality in the transmission of issues the elements of awareness and of consistency of direction of judgment with that taken by the convention itself or with the political action involved. The study judged efficiency in terms of the crystallization of opinion as well, and determined that the television group had a smaller "no opinion" segment than did either the radio or the newspaper group concerning the correctness of the action of the Republican convention in seating the Georgia delegation. The study did not test objectively the amount of the panel's increase of information concerning this issue, or set up any independent standard of judgment as to the correctness of the outcome.[20]

Simple tests of the correctness of information on important issues raised during the campaign were carried out, however, and it was concluded that in every instance these issues were better understood by those in the television audience than by those in the panel generally. But the newspaper was

---

reported only slightly greater gain in favorable opinion than the gains reported by those who followed the event on radio and in newspapers.

[18] " . . . it seems clear that Stevenson gained more than did Eisenhower from this medium. Part of this result stems from the lower level of recognition at which Stevenson began the campaign, and part appears to stem from the less friendly press, a matter of common awareness during the campaign. At any rate the gains in the evaluations made of the personal traits of Stevenson by those who relied on television must preclude certain relative gains which would have been expected for Eisenhower in this same group. The gains would have been anticipated for Eisenhower because of the analysis of the election itself which highlighted the importance of Eisenhower's personal characteristics and because of the properties of the television medium generally considered ideal for projecting these characteristics. In the final analysis, however, and on a relative basis, it can be said that Eisenhower gained the most in a personal way from the influence of newspapers and that Stevenson gained the most from the influence of television." The same, p. 47.

[19] The same, p. 48.

[20] The same, p. 49.

shown to be the superior instrument of communication for dealing with issues, despite the fact that those who watched on television thought they were making the largest gains of information.[21]

The over-all summary response of the panel showed that three-quarters of them thought television had influenced the election. Almost half of these believed this was so because of personal characteristics (people got to know the candidates personally; they got a better idea of mannerisms, facial expressions, and personal appearances). The remaining quarter thought so because people would rather watch than read. Forty-eight per cent of the panel thought Eisenhower had gained more from television than Stevenson did; 43.5 per cent were not sure which gained the more; and 8.5 per cent thought Stevenson profited more. Of those who thought the medium favored Eisenhower, 47.2 per cent gave personality reasons (sincerity, appearance, facial expressions, friendliness, humility, natural charm, fighting spirit, straightforwardness). Of those who thought the medium favored Stevenson, 80 per cent thought so because television helped him to become better known and to display his speaking ability.[22]

One important finding of the study was that most television impressions were made during the conventions and in the ten days preceding the election—times when personalities figured most prominently. And it was at these times that the bulk of voters' decisions were made. The apparent greater gains for Eisenhower hold true on an absolute basis, but when gains are measured relatively, Stevenson gained the more.[23]

But, the Miami group concluded, Eisenhower's absolute

[21] The same, p. 56.

[22] The same, pp. 56–57.

[23] The same, pp. 56–57. During the convention period, Eisenhower made a relative gain of 27.6 per cent; Stevenson, 36.7 per cent. Half way through the campaign Eisenhower was at a high point of 66.8 per cent preference in the panel; but during October he lost relatively among the television group, as Stevenson made a relative gain of 51.6 per cent (from absolute figures of 21.1 per cent to 32.0 per cent).

lead was too large. The decision of 1952 had already been made, and despite Stevenson's oncoming rush during the closing phases of the campaign, he could not overtake his opponent. "Under these circumstances, any influence of television could not possibly have been of a decisive nature. The results apparently would have been the same, with or without this new, and as yet untested, means of political communication."[24]

Campbell and his associates compared the influence of each of the main mass media on the campaign as a whole, and did not isolate coverage of the conventions. This report states the percentage of people who paid attention to the campaign via television, radio, newspapers, and magazines, classifying them by four geographic regions (Northeast, Midwest, South, Far West). It reports relative ratings of which media provided the most information on the campaign, and suggests influence of media by reporting the preferences of media among those who voted for Eisenhower, those who voted for Stevenson, and those who did not vote.

Campbell's nationwide figures show that television was cited as the source of most information on the campaign by more respondents (31 per cent) than any of the other media. But more people paid attention to the campaign through newspapers (79 per cent) and radio (69 per cent) than through television (53 per cent). Among those who voted for Eisenhower, magazines (54 per cent) and newspapers (44 per cent) led television (43 per cent) and radio (40 per cent) as the most important sources. Stevenson voters favored television (38 per cent), with newspapers (33 per cent), radio (25 per cent), and magazines (22 per cent) following in order.

Campbell and colleagues contented themselves with the conclusion that the influence of individual media was difficult to assess.[25] Further interpretation of their figures casts little

---

[24] The same, p. 64. See also p. 71.
[25] "Television and the Election," *Scientific American* (May 1953), p. 47.

general light on the impact of television. These data show that men rated television the most important source of information about the campaign; as many women preferred television as rated radio the most important. As to place of residence, television was rated most important in metropolitan areas, but in towns or cities, and in the open country, radio was the top medium. The more prosperous families (family income over $5,000 in 1952) rated television first, as did those in the $3,000–$5,000 bracket. But in the lower income group (less than $3,000) radio led substantially. It is in this bracket, of course, where the ability to buy a television set would operate most strongly as a determinant.

Among professional people, newspapers led television by a substantial margin, and magazines got their strongest preference. But among businessmen, managers, officials, clerical, sales and office workers, and skilled workers, television was rated the most important source. Unskilled workers preferred radio, and farmers put both radio and newspapers ahead of television.[26] In all of the foregoing, the conditions of the geography of television undoubtedly had an important effect in 1952—an effect that will be lessened in future years.

Two important recent studies of voting cast light on a phenomenon underlining the importance of the presentation of the convention and of pre-convention campaigning to the electorate, whether by television or by other media. One study notices that it is at the time of the conventions that many voters review their party preferences most actively and decide for whom they will vote in the forthcoming presidential election.[27] Campbell, Gurin, and Miller, in *The*

[26] The same, p. 48.
[27] Bernard R. Berelson, Paul F. Lazarsfeld, and William N. McPhee, *Voting* (1954), pp. 118–49; and their generalization No. 176, p. 345.

Voter Decides, have shown that in 1948 and in 1952, roughly one third of the voters had made up their minds before the conventions, and another third did so at the time of the conventions.[28]

Simon and Stern took advantage of the distribution of television stations and sets in Iowa in 1952, occasioned by the television freeze, to compare voting behavior of counties with a high density of television sets (HTD counties) to other counties. Their object was to see whether there were any significant differences (1) in voter turnout and (2) in preference for the Republican candidate. They also compared pairs of counties that had similar voting records in 1944 and 1948 but which differed in density of television set ownership in 1952, to see whether there were any differences on the same two counts. The authors found that their data did not "reveal any reliable difference either in the voting turnout or in the percentage of the vote cast for the Republican candidate between HTD and other areas."[29] On the hypothesis that interest was already high in Iowa, and therefore there was little room for television to drive participation higher or to cause shifts in party choice, the authors warned against generalizing their negative findings "to other types of campaigns."[30]

Accepting the caution of the authors about "other types

[28] Work cited, tables 2.4 and 2.5, pp. 18, 20. See also table 10.3, p. 150, which shows that more than a majority of all major subclasses of the sample studied (Eisenhower voters and Stevenson voters subclassified by predominant party identification, issue partisanship or candidate partisanship) had made up their minds at or before the time of the conventions, except Democrats who voted for Eisenhower. Thirty-nine per cent of the strong Democrats, and 47 per cent of the weak Democrats, had decided to vote for Eisenhower by the end of the conventions. The bulk of the remainder of weak Democrats decided for Eisenhower during the campaign. Twenty-six per cent of the strong Democrats decided for him at this time, but 28 per cent waited until two weeks before election day to make their choice, and 5 per cent decided on election day itself.

[29] *American Political Science Review*, Vol. 49, No. 2 (June 1955), p. 471.

[30] The same, p. 477.

of campaigns," and even extending it to the interpretation of the campaign in Iowa or to the presidential campaign as a whole in 1952, nevertheless, it seems unavoidable that television's ebullient claims of effectiveness in stimulating voter turnout are somewhat deflated by their findings. But, because the Simon-Stern study is an analysis of voting statistics, not based on observation or measurement of the course of development of political interest or choice in Iowa prior to election day, it casts little light on the efficiency of television in projecting personalities, clarifying issues, or in affecting other aspects of the campaign itself.[31] Thus it is impossible to use these findings to judge whether television helped Stevenson by making him known more rapidly than would otherwise have occurred, or whether Eisenhower made better use of television than Stevenson did, even in Iowa. The civic-mindedness and high literacy of Iowa would in any case reduce the value of data from this state as a guide to the effectiveness of television elsewhere.

As to turnout, the case of industry is highly plausible. Over 61.5 million voters turned out in 1952, as against 48.8 million in 1948; television was present in 18.5 million homes across the nation in 1952, but not in 1948; *Q.E.D.* But consideration of some earlier aspects of American presidential voting statistics, well before the advent of radio or of television, shows that turnout has jumped on past occasions without reference to marked changes in the communications environment. The most spectacular leap occurred, percentagewise, in 1840, when nearly twice as many voters turned out as had voted in 1836. Other significant leaps occurred from 1856 to 1860, when the Republican party was born (a jump from 4,054,000 to 5,680,000, a 40 per cent

---

[31] The authors' choice of mode of publication apparently constricted the description of their analytic model and a full estimate of the import of their data. Hence evaluation of the significance of their findings is hampered.

gain); again in 1896 with Bryan; and in 1916, when the vote came out that stayed at home in 1912. Over 8 million more votes were cast in 1920 than in 1916, a gain of better than one-third. Radio has already taken credit for the jump in 1928, which showed a gain of 7 millions over 1924, or about one-fourth greater. The gap between 1948 and 1952 was some 12,718,000 votes, or about 26 per cent.[32]

Inspection of a rough graph of voter turnout plotted as a percentage of the population of voting age also reveals that the rate of gain demonstrated in 1952 has been paralleled or exceeded at these earlier periods, in the absence of both radio and television.[33] This graph suggests one interpretation of voting statistics that may favor the claims of television. The rate of turnout decreases very sharply between 1916 and 1920 if the potential but unrealized women's vote is added to the potential voting population of 1920. Subsequent evidence suggests that the entry of women into presidential voting has been gradual, and it may be demonstrable by further analysis that television played a striking part in bringing out the women's vote in 1952.

This question still remains: Was it television, or something else, that jumped participation to 61.5 millions in 1952? And will the voting turnout of 1956 demonstrate a similar increase? The answer may reveal better data on which to estimate the effectiveness of the various media of communication in stimulating turnout and shaping decisions.

To summarize: the Simon-Stern study offers little information of relevance to the presidential nominating process, or to campaigning, but does throw into question the industry's claims of the importance of television in producing voter turnout. The studies of Campbell and others at the Michigan

[32] See U. S. Department of Commerce, *Statistical Abstract of the United States 1955*, Table No. 390, Historical Statistics of the United States, 1789–1945, Series P. 27–31, and *The World Almanac 1955*.

[33] Prepared by Richard Bain of the Brookings Institution.

Survey Center cast light on the time at which critical political choices are being made, indicating the importance of the
pre-convention and convention periods in 1948 and in 1952.
Only secondary information is available on the role of television in precipitating these choices or shifting preferences
oriented around party, candidate, or issue. The Miami study
is directly in point, verifying the Michigan findings that
in 1952 the critical choices were made early, and that the
conventions offered a decisive opportunity to affect voting
behavior. The Miami study also showed that transmission
of political content via television was not in itself a guarantee
of extensive, attentive, or efficient viewing. But none of the
studies cast any light on the relative objectivity with which
political events are viewed via television as compared to
other media. Industry claims of this nature must continue
to rest on grounds of plausibility. Studies that adequately
measure the political impact of television, whether emerging
from conventions or from other political events, have yet
to be made.

Growth and Changes in the
Medium After 1952

The growth of television from 1952 to the present has
been enormously important both numerically and geographically. By the middle of 1954, the number of sets had
jumped from 18 millions to over 30 millions, almost all in
homes. And the distribution over previously uncovered
areas of the country had thickened markedly. These processes continued. As revealed by a census of television in
homes taken in June 1955,[34] there were 32,106,000 households in which there was at least one television set; that is,
television was found in 67.2 per cent of all households in the

[34] *National Survey of Television Sets in U. S. Households—June 1955.* Conducted by
the Bureau of the Census for the Advertising Research Foundation.

country. Television-set density varied with urbanization: 78.3 per cent of households inside standard metropolitan areas had television; 55.9 per cent of households in urban places outside metropolitan areas; and 45.9 per cent of households in rural territory outside metropolitan areas. The industry estimated the total of sets in use would grow to 42 millions by July 1, 1956, and the total number of sets would then approximate the number of families now in the television area—43,600,000, or 91 per cent of all families in the United States. The industry also estimated that 71 per cent of all homes would have television in 1956, and most of them would have access to network programs.[35]

With the freeze ended in the summer of 1952, the number of stations jumped to 371 in 234 market areas[36] by July 1,

[35] Special tabulation prepared by NBC: testimony of Joseph V. Heffernan, Financial Vice President, NBC, April 1955, before the Senate Subcommittee on Privileges and Elections of the Committee on Rules and Administration.

[36] The term "market areas," so common in television statistics because of the relation of broadcasting to marketing, is based on official classifications of metropolitan and other areas by the U. S. Bureau of the Census and certain other federal agencies. As used, for example, by the J. Walter Thompson Company, market areas are defined and classified into metropolitan markets (i.e., metropolitan areas); smaller urban markets; and farm markets, as follows:

"162 metropolitan markets:

    8 A   markets—population over 2,000,000.
  35 B   markets—population 450,000 to 2,000,000.
  72 C   markets—population 150,000 to 450,000.
  47 D' markets—population 50,000 to 150,000.
436 smaller urban markets:

  150 D markets—counties with one or more cities with a population between 25,000 and 50,000.
  286 E markets—counties with no cities with populations over 25,000 but having populations of which more than 50 per cent is urban in character. (Urban population is that which lives in incorporated or unincorporated places of 2,500 population or more.)
      F' markets—counties with above average farm income.
      F markets—counties with below average farm income."

These figures are based on the census of 1950. The 162 metropolitan markets approximate the 168 metropolitan areas defined in that census. (The difference exists because of the fact that the advertising analysis defines metropolitan markets in New England according to county, not township lines, and includes Newport News in the Norfolk-Portsmouth area.) J. Walter Thompson Company, *Population and Its Distribution*, 7th ed. (1951).

1954. Since that time the expected rate of growth in stations has dropped somewhat. *Television Digest* lists 451 stations on the air or due to be on the air by the end of 1955 in continental United States; additional stations in Alaska (4), Hawaii (5), and Puerto Rico (2) bring the total to 462.[37] The industry is constructing "booster" stations, which will simultaneously broadcast programs originating in stronger stations to give fuller coverage to those areas not now receiving a good television signal. These developments mean that, in 1956, there will be solid television coverage in every important metropolitan area in the country.

The great majority of metropolitan areas will be able to choose from at least two stations. At present, in the top 100 television market areas, 17 are served by one station, 36 by two, 33 by three, and 14 by four or more stations.[38] In 1952, there were 41 one-station outlets in which the station had a choice of network service.[39]

The growth of television will go far to reduce the comparative advantage of radio in giving uniform coverage to the country as a whole. This comparative advantage has been marked to date. Arthur C. Nielsen described the situation in 1953 as follows:

Radio still follows population distribution evenly in its regional pattern. TV does not, showing a variation in degree of saturation that

[37] See insert map, Television Stations and Network Routes: 1955, accompanying *Television Factbook*, No. 21 (Fall–Winter, 1955).

[38] Ted Bergmann, "Dumont to be Film Network Using New, Fast Process," *Broadcasting-Telecasting* (Apr. 18, 1955), p. 28. This article reports progress in the Electronicam process for simultaneous filming and television pickup, which makes it possible to get high-fidelity film recording at the same time that a television image is shot. It requires standard studio lighting, and apparently makes possible network coverage for most subjects other than sports, special events, or hot news. It simplifies editing, and is relatively cheap if the daily cost of using the camera (some $6,700) can be spread over several subjects.

[39] *Television Factbook*, No. 15 (July 15, 1952), pp. 9–25. The count excludes Albuquerque, which was not yet on the coaxial cable or able to pick up network programs by microwave. It includes Newark, which was technically a one-station market although most viewers in the area could get service from the various New York stations.

ranged from 77 per cent in the North East, to 36 per cent in the South. Similarly, radio's distribution by county size is far more even than TV's, the latter tending to concentrate in the large, metropolitan counties and being relatively weak in the small, rural ones.[40]

The quality of the signal may be somewhat improved, just as the average quality of home receivers may rise. The major advance will be toward color television. The expectations of the industry concerning color in early 1955 were very optimistic, looking to growth from 5,000 color sets in the hands of users in mid-1954 to a million such sets in mid-1956. However, this number still means that only 2 per cent of all homes in the United States, out of a possible 82 per cent that lie within the color transmission area, would have color sets.[41] And the number of color sets in use as of June 30, 1955, was only 8,000.[42]

Obviously, with this growth in the number and distribution of television sets and stations, television audiences have increased and will continue to do so. By January 1953, when the first presidential inauguration was carried coast to coast on television, the station list had grown to 118 in 75 cities, and an estimated 75 million viewers saw at least some part of the ceremonies. This is the largest political audience to date, but could easily be surpassed by the forthcoming audiences for the 1956 conventions and election events. The 1954 elections, however, dealing with congressional and state politics primarily, do not seem to have excited the same amount of interest as did the national spectacle.

As noticed above, the conventions seem to have outdrawn "normal" television, especially during daytime hours. Some other political events seem to have a similar attraction. The McCarthy-Army hearings boosted daytime audiences by 53

---

[40] *Broadcasting-Telecasting*, 1954 Broadcasting Yearbook/Market-book issue, p. 16.
[41] Special tabulation, NBC.
[42] *Television Factbook*, No. 21 (Fall–Winter, 1955), p. 19, quoting *Sylvania* research estimates.

per cent over normal.[43] The conclusion seems inescapable from available data that politics on the national scale makes popular television.

[43] *Broadcasting-Telecasting* (May 10, 1954), p. 57. Trendex figures showed that a combined audience of the two New York television stations carrying the hearings was 59.8 per cent of the total audience. Hooperatings bore out these findings in Boston, New York, Milwaukee, and Houston.

CHAPTER IV

The National Conventions of 1956—
Plans and Problems

SIMPLE extrapolation of the experience through 1952, corrected to take account of the growth of television and any foreseeable technical changes in it, will not suffice to indicate the impact of television on the nominating process in 1956—and is even less adequate as applied to the longer future. It is already clear that the conventions in 1956 will differ notably from those of 1952 or 1948. The role of television as reporter, analyst, and commentator will perforce be different, and its political effects will undoubtedly be modified also. The discussion below relates current political and technical expectations for 1956 to the range of possibilities revealed by experience to date, and offers some speculation on how experience in 1956 may change matters for the future.

The Political Setting

Plans made and political possibilities estimated prior to September 1955 for the forthcoming conventions, as they relate to television, were founded on the expectations (1) that the most likely nominees were well known in advance; and (2) the conventions were likely to be relatively peaceful. Decisions had already been taken to hold the conventions in widely separated cities, one following immediately after the other.

The Democratic convention will precede the Republican for the first time since 1888. The Democrats will gather in

Chicago and start their formal convention proceedings on Monday, August 13. The Republicans open a week later in San Francisco, on Monday, August 20, and plan to meet from 2 to 7 P.M. Pacific time each day.

Prior to the President's heart attack, it appeared that Eisenhower and Stevenson could again have the two nominations if they wanted them, although there was a minority sentiment that both parties might pick new leaders in 1956. The capacity of television as candidate-maker had as yet produced no surprises. But with the President's illness, events took an unexpected and puzzling turn. It immediately became far more doubtful whether the President would accept the nomination again, even if he were physically able to do so. Speculation ran rife in the Republican party as to whom, if anyone, the President might choose as heir apparent. Republican jockeying for position increased, although hampered by the President's understandable withholding of any statement about his intentions which might reduce his influence in the party or as the country's leader; until the President had spoken, no one would wish to run afoul of his popularity or risk his displeasure. Yet the enhanced prospect that the President would not run made it important for candidates to prepare their positions if the way should open up. The whole picture was further complicated, as the months wore on and the President's health steadily improved, by the efforts of those Republicans who refused to accept the possibility that Eisenhower would not be available. In the Democratic party, the new turn of events fostered overt moves toward capturing the candidacy, as the value of the nomination rose with the possibility that the Republican opponent might be weaker than the President.

In any case, the President's illness changed basically the situation that the Republican party faced. Now there is considerable prospect of a real fight for the nomination, accentuating and dramatizing the splits in the party, and the convention may well be an exciting event. And with the outcome difficult to predict, the impact on the subsequent Republican campaign might well be considerable. Given a continuation of prosperity and a reduction of international tension, this impact could be small; an intervening depression or international crisis might raise controversy to the point where all the vaunted facilities of modern communications would be strained to present to the people the official policies of the party in the short time remaining after the selection of the nominee and the firming up of policy choices and campaign strategies. It does not appear, however, that the Republican convention will produce much public controversy over its platform in any case. Despite the deep split in the Republican ranks, the party has not often engaged in open controversy over platform issues at its recent conventions. Moreover, the Republican convention will not have the task of preparing a platform attacking a party in power, but must defend its political record and give assurances and create positive expectations for the future. Fights in the credentials committee, if they occur, may provide more drama.

The Democratic convention offers greater prospect of dramatic disagreement. Their nomination fight may be more colorful and the party disagreements more open. Their platform activities can be more exciting than those of the Republicans, but novelty will be lessened by the fact that the Democrats dominate Congress. Thus they bear some responsibility for government programs, and at the same time must make a day-by-day record of criticism of the administration. The conventions can summarize and dramatize these things, but any significant new attacks can be met by the countercharge that during the preceding two years, the Democrats did little about them.

More significant than the foregoing, however, could be

the effect on Democratic strategy, choice of candidate, and policies if the President does not run, if there is no Republican heir apparent with an odds-on chance for the nomination, and if the Democrats must adjust themselves to a Republican strategy that they cannot fully foresee.

The fact that the parties have already chosen different convention cities and placed their conventions much later in the year, has significance both for party strategy in the campaigns and for television operations. The parties realized afresh in 1952 how useful the conventions could be for campaigning. With massive costs of television and the prospect of a large audience temporarily deprived of choice of television fare, the value of convention time bulked large as a free bonanza, calling for the most efficient utilization. And with closer juxtaposition to the traditionally serious campaigning period after Labor Day, it can be expected that the parties will make special efforts to relate convention proceedings to their conduct of the campaign. Television may be used more to project issues, especially if the candidates are already well known, and if the parties use some creative imagination in exploiting the visual resources of television.

From the standpoint of television, the expected physical arrangements present novel and difficult problems. Part of these problems are logistical, part are editorial. To begin with, the decision to meet in separate cities practically eliminated color transmission. It was simply too expensive to set up in two locations, for the number of color viewers. Problems for black-and-white transmission are serious, too. Even if the Democratic convention is a short one, the networks cannot safely plan to use the same equipment to cover both conventions. They must have duplicate equipment on hand in both cities, and may have to cover the conventions with smaller facilities than would be available for conventions in a single city. These difficulties are mitigated somewhat by the fact that television has enormous producing facilities already available on the West Coast, centered around Los Angeles. In any case, the networks will have to set up large temporary installations twice instead of once, obviously at greater expense for a given level of equipment. Lucrative sponsorship will therefore appear more attractive than ever.

These geographical separations and the time overlap will strain personnel even more than equipment. Previously, the networks moved all available man power, technical and editorial, to the convention city. Now they must divide their forces, at least for a time, between two fronts.

Editorial problems present more difficulties than those of logistics. The networks must decide how to cover Democratic proceedings that will still be under way at the same time that they report the preliminaries of the Republican convention—preliminaries that may well be highly newsworthy. No one can tell in advance whether the Democratic convention proceedings will be dull at the right moments to allow the networks to switch their pictures to the Republican committee preliminaries without loss of continuity, interest, and important substance of one or the other event.

Technically the problem of dual coverage is not insuperable. It is possible for each network to cover both events and give to a central editor the responsibility of deciding which picture to select. But if coverage were so pooled, the result would be to diminish the opportunity of the viewer to select the event he wishes to watch. If the networks agree on some mutually convenient division of labor, the choice of the viewer can be widened, but at the same time there will arise additional questions of relations with commercial sponsors, relative advantage in terms of audience building and public service, and possible expression of political preference. The most costly and editorially difficult solution would be for each network to cover each event fully, and to exercise continuing choice as to which event to put on the air. Such a solution would give the viewer some range of choice, although short of the maximum he would enjoy if he could choose between full live coverage of both events.

The Democrats will have a clear field for their pre-convention preliminaries, and have the advantage of initial position. Telecasting of their convention itself may be blurred by coverage of the Republican preliminaries, but in competition between the two it is likely that the kinds of decisions being taken by the Democrats will be of more interest to the public than the relatively technical preliminaries being conducted by the Republicans. In other words, the final stages of candidate selection at the Democratic convention will be more generally comprehensible and newsworthy than the intra-party maneuverings for delegate seats—a part of the business, moreover, that the Republican managers were least willing to have televised in 1952.

The Republicans have the advantage of closer proximity to the subsequent campaign, but must bear the disadvantage of presenting their convention during the third week of convention television, when the interest of the audience may be jaded.

Revision of Convention Procedures

The presence of television at the 1952 conventions helped precipitate immediate changes in the Republican rules, and led to action by both parties that will significantly alter convention procedure in 1956 and in the future. Television highlighted the basic problems of how to settle contests over delegate seating, how to integrate plenary sessions with convention committee action, and how and under what conditions to permit roll call votes and the individual polling of delegations. In the Republican convention, the Langlie "fair play" amendment dealing with seating of contested delegations was adopted first as a temporary measure, and later in the convention incorporated into the permanent rules as Section 4f. The Republicans also established new procedures to investigate credentials contests in advance of the conventions, which might reduce the amount of linen-washing in front of television audiences in the future. In the Democratic convention, there had been several instances in which the chairman seemed to misapply the cumbersome rules of the convention, governing when a roll call vote should be taken.[1] Roll calls as such were a first-class nuisance in both conventions, and in the Democratic convention they were the worse because of fractional voting. The Democrats had their problem too of what to do with their "so-called or miscalled Loyalty Pledge Resolution." The result was that the Democratic National Committee, in 1953, established a special advisory committee on rules and procedure for the 1956 Democratic National Convention.[2]

In more detail, the Republican changes were as follows: First, they adopted the heart of the Langlie proposal to prevent a contested delegate or delegates from voting in the con-

[1] For example, Dever's decisions on demands for a roll call vote early Tuesday morning, on the Daniels amendment to the Moody resolution, and on the Moody resolution itself. He claimed without a count that one-fifth of the delegates had not arisen, and declared the former matter defeated and the second passed by a voice vote. See Paul T. David, Malcolm Moos, Ralph M. Goldman, *Presidential Nominating Politics in 1952*, Vol. I (1954), pp. 125–27. A further example was Rayburn's controversial decision on Thursday to entertain an appeal from the ruling of the chair on seating Virginia, quickly noticing that one-fifth of the delegates had demanded a roll call vote and proceeding to hold it, when there seems to have been no adequate demand or preparation for it. The same, pp. 141–42.

[2] This committee submitted a report entitled *Interim Report of Special Advisory Committee on Rules of the 1956 Democratic National Convention* (hereinafter cited as *Interim Report*) on June 8, 1955, which was published by the Democratic National Committee shortly thereafter, and approved unanimously by the committee in Chicago on Nov. 17, 1955. See Gould Lincoln, "4,640 Convention Seats Approved by Democrats," *The Evening Star*, Washington, D. C. (Nov. 18, 1955). The report will be submitted to the national convention in 1956 for its adoption or change.

vention or in any committee thereof until permanently seated by the convention,[3] unless placed on the temporary roll by at least a two-thirds vote of the national committee. Another change empowered the national committee to take jurisdiction over seating contests arising out of the irregular or unlawful action of a state committee or state convention. A third permitted governing Republican committees of states or territories to prescribe after due public notice qualifications not inconsistent with law for participants in state or local party gatherings, in addition to qualifications prescribed in the national convention rules.[4]

A long, detailed, and possibly more important new provision dealt with the procedure for preparing contests to be heard by the national committee. The convention established a new, special seven-man contest committee to receive from competing factions statements of the basis of contests well in advance of the convention; and to work up clear statements of the issues of fact and law for the consideration of the national committee and subsequently, if necessary, of the convention itself. The new rule also tightened up procedure for consideration of contests by the national committee, the credentials committee, and the convention.[5] This procedure, depending largely on the quality of the chairman of the contest committee and his colleagues, could do much to increase the order and judicial quality of deciding delegate contests, and to eliminate frivolous or unnecessary ones.[6]

Under established Republican procedures, the consideration of delegate contests can begin well before the conven-

---

[3] Republican National Convention, *Official Proceedings* (1952), p. 281.

[4] The same, pp. 279, 280.

[5] The same, pp. 293–94.

[6] It is worth pointing out that a party convention is a parliamentary body, and that the action on contested delegations does not turn simply on issues of law and equity. The purpose of the party is victory, and the implied requirement is party strength and unity. Even if the contest committee is not primarily mindful of these matters, the national committee and the convention must be.

tion. Members of the credentials committee are to be chosen by state delegates as soon as the latter are elected. These choices are to be reported to the national committee immediately. Then, in the case of delegate contests, the national committee notifies them, and they have the right to attend all hearings of all contests before the national committee, but without vote.[7] Thus the members of the credentials committee of the convention have the opportunity to familiarize themselves thoroughly with the nature of the facts, the issues, and the political values of each contest in advance of the actual meeting of the convention. This form of procedure makes it possible for the credentials committee of the convention to co-ordinate action in the convention with that in the national committee, but it by no means affords any guarantee that the outcome on contested delegations will be the same. The Republican experience in 1952, when the action of the convention overturned the decisions of the national committee and the credentials committee, furnishes eloquent proof.[8]

Further changes in the Republican rules may be recommended by a committee appointed by the Republican National Committee under the chairmanship of Governor McKeldin; these cannot now be adumbrated with sufficient clarity to permit appraisal of their impact on television and conventions of the future.[9] But it is certain that the problems exacerbated by television will come under the scrutiny of the committee.

The Democratic special advisory committee on rules has already come up with concrete proposals, unanimously approved by the national committee on November 17, 1955,

[7] Rule 4(d). The same, p. 294.
[8] See David, Moos, Goldman, *Presidential Nominating Politics in 1952*, Vol I, pp. 79 ff.
[9] Letter to Paul T. David from Governor Theodore R. McKeldin, Dec. 9, 1955. The Republican rules committee does not plan to report to the national committee until the convention meets in San Francisco.

that affect procedure for delegation polling and taking roll calls, and that may streamline convention action by shifting most of the work of the important convention committees into the week preceding the convention. Proceeding on a memorandum from Stephen A. Mitchell, John S. Battle, and Hubert Humphrey, which pointed out that "the 1952 abuse of the polling privilege by TV-hungry delegates indicates a change in the rule is desirable," the committee recommended a revised rule as follows:

Rule 5. (a) On roll call by States, a delegation shall be polled on challenge by any member of the delegation; and

(b) The Convention Chairman may send a representative to the delegation to conduct the poll; and in the discretion of the Convention Chairman, the roll call may continue instead of awaiting the result of the polling; and

(c) The determination of the Chairman's representative of the results of the poll so challenged, shall be spread upon the records of the Convention, and shall be conclusive unless an open poll in the hearing of the entire Convention is demanded by one-third of the delegates of the State involved; and

(d) A demand for poll may be withdrawn at any time. In the event a demand for poll is withdrawn, the vote announced by the Chairman of the delegation will stand unchallenged, but the Convention Chairman's representative shall offer other members of the delegation opportunity to request continuance of the poll.[10]

The advisory committee also considered and rejected suggestions that delegations should be removed from the convention floor while being polled. The grounds for rejection were these: such removal was objectionable in principle, since no business of the convention should be conducted when a delegation is compelled by the convention to be physically absent; and it was judged that the noise and confusion of a departure from and return to the convention floor would be considerable and might conflict with some other important activity.[11]

[10] *Interim Report*, pp. 9, 39.

[11] The same, pp. 9–10. Chairman Butler, in his letter of transmittal of the report to members of the national committee, expressed hope that this proposal would get further consideration. The same, p. 1.

The intent of the newly adopted provisions is to make it more difficult for a few delegates to hold up proceedings for a poll, while protecting the right of every delegate to call for an independent check on the vote as announced by the chairman of this delegation. These objectives may or may not be gained. The convention chairman may decide to poll the delegation in public, even if the one-third requirement is not met. He may wish to use up, not save, time. And the one-third requirement is by no means a high hurdle to a delegation determined to get television attention: 17 delegations in 1956 will number 30 or less half-votes. Furthermore, a delegation chairman anxious to be counted at the right time in a roll call may press at least a third of his delegates to demand a poll rather than let the choice of a smaller number postpone his announced vote until the end of the roll call that is expected to reveal the choice of the convention. If delegations—especially the large ones—are determined to filibuster, the rule is of no avail against them, and the prospects of delay in polling a delegation of 196 members and 110 alternates are formidable. But by the same token the one-third figure goes up substantially, and with it the prospect that substantial time-saving can be made.[12]

Polls and roll calls are closely connected; one way to avoid delegation polling is to avoid roll calls, preferably by doing the preparatory work in committee so well that it does not have to be done over in the convention. Roll calls presumably will always be necessary in the actual making of presidential

---

[12] The "TV-hunger" of the average delegate is, of course, an imponderable. But it may well remain high. Most delegates are party workers, for whom the choice as delegate and the opportunity to participate in the party's convention is a reward for faithful and little-recognized service. Thus they are not accustomed to the attentions of mass media, whether in the form of newspaper interviews or of appearances on radio and television. A poll will furnish in the future as today a chance to put one's Hitchcock into the picture; to remind onlookers at home of one's presence; or to demonstrate to local leaders the faithful performance of a trust. In a sense, it may provide reinsurance if an unorthodox vote is extracted by an obviously bulldozing delegation chairman; television provides something of a safeguard against such tactics.

nominations, but for every other issue, the demand for a roll call vote is a sign of the inadequacy of previous committee work or of the unrepresentativeness of the committee in which the work was conducted. There is also value in reducing the ambiguity of the circumstances under which a convention presiding officer can authorize a roll call (*i.e.*, the demand of one-fifth of the delegates present).

The special advisory committee recommended a further rule change, as follows: "Rule 7. Roll calls should be taken upon the demand of eight delegations."[13] Such a rule should obviously reduce the discretion of the chairman in ordering roll calls, and will make slightly more difficult than does the Republican rule (a call by six delegations) a convention decision to take them.

A major difficulty in the timing and execution of the business of a convention, complicated considerably by the presence of television, has been the work of the major convention committees concurrent with that of the convention itself. One result in the past has been "dull Tuesday"—a period when the official opening ceremonies are over and the keynote speech is out of the way, but the working committees of the convention are not yet ready to report. The action of the special advisory committee on this matter was as follows:

In order to improve and modernize the procedures of the Convention, the Advisory Committee recommends that the Democratic National Committee adopt certain procedures in advance of the opening of the 1956 Convention, in the expectation of cooperation from the individuals and groups affected, and of formal approval by the Convention in due course.

The Advisory Committee gave careful consideration to the practical necessity for attendance at the Convention city, in advance of the opening of the Convention, of the members of the

---

[13] *Interim Report*, p. 10. The Mitchell-Battle-Humphrey memorandum recommended that roll calls be taken on the demand of six delegations; a rule "easier to administer, without controversy, than the present rule providing for roll calls upon the demand of one-fifth of the delegates present." The same, p. 39.

(1) Committee on Permanent Organization
(2) Committee on Rules and Order of Business
(3) Committee on Credentials
(4) Committee on Resolutions and Platform

The Advisory Committee recognized that the members of these committees are chosen by the State Delegations and determined that it would be practical for the State Delegations to nominate their members, at least seven days in advance of the opening of the Convention. This would permit the members of the committees to meet during the week prior to the opening of the convention, so they could do their work under less pressure and more satisfactory conditions. This advance work could be accomplished, and would shorten the preliminary phases of the Convention and bring many other benefits, if the members of these committees met as *de facto* bodies without waiting their formal organization as *de jure* bodies, by the confirmation of the Convention. Accordingly, the Committee by majority vote, recommends:

"Rule 8. That the Democratic National Committee request the State Delegations to make their nominations at *least* seven days in advance of the opening of the Convention, for members of the following Committees:

"Committee on Permanent Organization
"Committee on Rules and Order of Business
"Committee on Credentials
"Committee on Resolutions and Platform

"Rule 9. That the members of the foregoing committees meet in the Convention City on a call of the Chairman of the Democratic National Committee, at times and places determined by him, at any time during the week prior to the opening of the Convention, and proceed with the work of the respective committees as *de facto* bodies, in anticipation of labor [*sic*; later?] confirmation as *de jure* committees by action of the Convention."[14]

As we have already noted, Republican procedure already permits this preparatory work, but has not always resulted in a streamlining of convention business. The Democrats may be more successful; in any case, if they adopt the device, the opportunity is there. The new move is not without its special problems; the question whether to have these preliminary meetings open to the press (all of it) may be more difficult to answer in practice than by doctrinal principle, whenever any

[14] The same, pp. 10–11.

serious controversy is afoot or radical adjustment of factional differences is being sought.

One further reform, not yet under serious consideration by either party, might work toward avoidance of floor battles over matters that have been previously decided by the national committee of either party or their convention committees. This would make the convention committees more representative of the conventions to which they report, by some such device as allocating seats in the committees proportional to the delegation votes in the convention. Thus, while every state would have at least one representative (or two, if necessary to equate sexes) the larger states would have additional representatives for, say, each twelve convention votes. This would tend to avoid reversed voting; *i.e.*, the situation in which a result is arrived at on the basis of one-state one-vote in the committees, but is overturned on the floor when the states previously outvoted are able to bring their full weight into play. An example of this overturn was the vote on seating the Georgia delegation in the Republican 1952 convention.[15]

Further proposals for change adopted by the Democratic National Committee in approving the report of the special advisory committee included a new form of loyalty pledge, a provision that delegates on the temporary roll of the convention may not vote on their own credentials, and a somewhat improved procedure for hearing credentials contests. All of these would tend to reduce the amount of friction and controversy at the convention itself, thereby making it a faster and more orderly but possibly less colorful and in-

[15] Both the national committee and the convention credentials committee had voted to seat the pro-Taft Georgia delegation, the latter by a vote of 30–21. The minority report was signed by 22 states and the Virgin Islands. Losers in the credentials committee, these states came from delegations with a total strength of 646 votes (convention majority: 604). These delegations provided 532 of the 607 votes by which the pro-Eisenhower Georgia delegation was seated by the convention. See David, Moos, Goldman, *Presidential Nominating Politics in 1952*, Vol. I, pp. 77–84.

teresting event. The form of certification of loyalty relied on good faith in the action of state Democratic parties in selecting and certifying delegates to the Democratic National Convention, and chose to interpret the very process of becoming delegates as adequate assurance that those certified by state Democratic parties are bona fide Democrats having the interests, welfare, and success of the party at heart, who will participate in the convention in good faith. Therefore no additional assurances should be required of them in the absence of credentials contest or challenge.[16]

Noted but not officially sanctioned were proposals to replace speeches by forums and panels, to allow short acceptance speeches by nominees, to limit "demonstrations" to fifteen minutes, and suggestions to the chairman to fill idle periods by calling on distinguished Democrats for short statements not exceeding two or three sentences.[17]

Equally or more important for the decorum, procedure, and character of the conventions of 1956 than the foregoing procedural changes were the decisions of both national committees to increase the number of delegates over that of the 1952 conventions. The official Republican representation was raised only slightly; the official number of delegates became 1,323 for 1956 against 1,206 for 1952, and the Republican procedure of allowing one alternate per delegate resulted in a maximum official delegation of 2,646. But the Democrats did far more. They raised the official delegate vote total from 1,230 to 1,372, and their policy of allowing half-votes and their method of figuring number of alternates raised the total number of delegates to 2,744, and of alternates to 1,896—a whopping total of 4,640.[18] Television might help by reducing the demands for spectator space, more than ever

---

[16] *Interim Report*, pp. 8–9.
[17] The same, pp. 39–40.
[18] Gould Lincoln, "Both Parties Increase Convention Delegations," *The Evening Star*, Washington, D. C. (Dec. 11, 1955), p. A-4.

at a premium as the alternates cut into gallery seating. But the prospect of crowded aisles, overpopulous demonstrations, excessive noise, and, above all, confusion in the voting was greatly enhanced.

Development of Equipment

At present writing, the main technological developments that may affect convention coverage and its probable impact have to do with ultra high frequency transmission, with color television, and with improved facilities for covering events both in the hall and in the areas of remote pickups.

The potential impact of ultra high frequency (UHF) bears mainly on the question of the nationwide distribution of television coverage. UHF does not now offer any points of technological superiority over VHF in range of coverage by any one station or in quality of picture; it may be less efficient in these respects. But use of UHF may increase somewhat total coverage of television by increasing the number of stations, while it sharpens competition among existing television outlets. Although UHF appears necessary to provide fully nationwide television service within the limitations of the electromagnetic spectrum, it is not now expected that by 1956 UHF will greatly increase the total area in which television can be received; but it can increase the area in which a multiplicity of pictures is available. UHF may offer reason to hope, simply because of greater competition, that new and more imaginative methods of treating the conventions as news events may be developed.

Expected increases in stations, both UHF and VHF, and in receiving sets make it more than likely that the political strategist considering how to use television in 1956 can assume coverage of every important metropolitan area in the nation, and a considerable increase in smaller urban areas and in rural coverage as well. For the longer future, a major avenue of development leads toward saturation of rural as well as of metropolitan areas, although movement in this direction is impeded by the economics of television, which tend to concentrate the medium in the most populous and profitable marketing areas. The question of how rural saturation would affect the nominating process depends, of course, on the effect of television on political figures and groups not now reached by television, and their role in the nominating process itself.

Color television was not a factor in 1952 or in 1954; the number of stations that could originate color and the number of sets that could receive color were very small. But color may be an important factor in 1956 from the point of view of the industry, although as of November 1955 the networks were not planning to cover the conventions in color. If color is used, however, the conventions offer tempting opportunities as a spectacular event to demonstrate the superiority of one or another form of color transmission, and to gain in the competitive race against other media bidding for the advertiser's dollar. Color transmission may affect convention managements and delegates, because color equipment is bulkier and heavier, and requires more intense and better balanced lighting than does black-and-white television. It will certainly complicate the logistical problems of the industry. It is doubtful whether the psychological impact of color transmission on the viewer would be appreciably different, from a political point of view, from the impact of black-and-white.

More efficient cameras and microphones are being developed and may have some effect. Today's "creepie-peepie" can give a much better picture than was possible in 1952. Therefore convention managements are confronted by a problem: whether to allow them freely on the floor at all times, in order to provide a more varied and intimate picture of proceedings, or whether to keep them off the floor in the interest

of better order in the hall, to reduce the appearance of confusion and indiscipline, and to minimize risks of injudicious
action or speech on the part of delegates or their managers.
Confusion and risks will be increased considerably, since
freedom of the floor to the creepie-peepies means freedom of
the floor to walkie-talkies and to still photographers. The
demonstrated possibilities of crowding and confusion are considerable. A compromise that would open the floor during
periods of slack movement but close it during periods of
serious and active business, might be adopted.

Better microphones open up considerable possibilities for
coverage of the convention event as a whole. The Agronsky
incident suggests what might happen when an ostensibly
secret meeting is being spied on. A more sensitive microphone might have allowed him to pick up the actual sound of
the delegates arguing, as well as the visual picture.

The combination of better sight and sound coverage will
help operators to get around and to multiply the number of
images available for choice by the originating sources. But
aside from greater efficiency in penetrating secret places, the
initial effect will be simply to multiply details. Whether they
can be woven into a more meaningful whole depends on the
development of the editorial and reporting process itself.

Dumont's development of a simultaneous high-fidelity
filming and telecasting operation may lengthen the duration
of effective television coverage of convention events by providing more high-quality footage worth later repetition. But
this development is not yet fast enough to affect immediate
operations.

Developments in News Presentation

What developments are taking place or are in prospect in
the fields of political news reporting and coverage that

have implications for 1956 and for the longer future of the nominating process? Conversations with network officials and newsmen do not indicate any important changes, present or future. The objectives of the newsmen remain the same: to uncover and report what is newsworthy by commonly accepted (and slowly developing) American journalistic standards. The bizarre will always have a place, but there seems to be an increasing reliance on reporting the well-defined central stream of an event. Newsmen will continue to fight, whether working for television, radio, or any other news medium, for entree into any place where they believe that important facets of their story are developing. They will come as close as ingenuity, conscience, and the demands of news judgment and editorial discretion will allow in making the full details available to the public.[19] Television and radio will continue as in the past to emphasize their advantage over other media in reporting more promptly than their competitors the outcome of the vote, the race, or the platform decision. They will continue to crowd the printed media in

[19] There is no intention to imply that newsmen are without conscience. They have strong consciences, animated chiefly by the moral virtue of getting and publishing all relevant details of any story in which they are concerned. But the moral value in our society of open reporting of anything of general significance or interest—in particular, political events such as party decisions or choices—operates strongly to override other values, such as respect for the privacy of individuals. When the issue is clouded by the argument that secret caucuses are mainly valuable for the reputation and power of the party, it is difficult to assert the countervalue that any institution such as a political party needs the opportunity to assess its interests and arrange its strategies and co-ordinate its forces in secret. Even the striking example of the Constitutional Convention—held in secret, on issues of utmost concern to the body politic, but nevertheless honorable, respectable, wise, and durable in outcome—is difficult to establish as a precedent for secrecy for a subordinate organization of a political party against the newsman's onslaughts. Given the variety of values involved, which is only suggested here, it is not surprising that there is considerable range in the behavior of newsmen concerning what they feel free to report or not to report. At one end of the continuum is the newsman who respects no confidences or deadlines, and only promises co-operation as a means of getting a story, which he intends to reveal as promptly as possible, preferably ahead of his colleagues. At the other stand the many newsmen who have been entrusted with the most vital secrets of military or diplomatic character, and have been scrupulously honest about observing their pledges.

their "depth coverage," with radio under special pressure to emphasize the work of the commentator or analyst.[20] Television, as a visual medium, may make further inroads into the printed media, although it will not, for the ordinary viewer and in the immediate future, provide the service of record that is so well done by newspaper and magazine. The future may see developments in which even this advantage is overcome, if such innovations as Telefax (an instrument for the electronic transmission of a printed message) are cheapened to the point where they can be widely installed in homes.

Competition among media is not the whole story, however. As politicians well know, media reinforce one another. What is seen on television is often read about in newspapers and magazines with heightened impact and increased transmission of information. Newspapers allow their readers to pick up what they have missed on television. And television shows (such as "Meet the Press" or "Face the Nation") often provide headlines and stories of more than transient importance. Radio remains of great value. With over 100 million sets in use, it is still the greatest medium of communication. It is notably useful in daytime programs for women. Speeches are better adapted to radio than to television. With appropriate technical imagination—such as the use of multiple voices to avoid monotony—radio retains freshness and interest. And there are situations in which the

[20] As radio loses ground in the competitive race with television as a medium for advertising, radio may be freed for more responsible and imaginative employment. Radio is stressing today its growing role in local community affairs. At present writing, it appears that radio is holding a place in the advertisers' budgets and the communicators' interests because it is still the more widely distributed medium. Not only geographically, but in the home as well, radio is found in more rooms. And radio is feasible in automobiles and places where a visual medium would be impractical or unsafe. Fundamental is the observation that it is possible to do other things while listening to radio. This compatibility with other functions offers an avenue for the development of radio as a mature medium of intelligent discussion as well as of music and reportage. Conceivably this compatibility may more than overcome the inability of radio to combine a visual image with its power to speak.

free visual fantasy of the listener is politically a more valuable accompaniment than the possibly restrictive or distracting effect of television visual shots.

Coverage of the 1954 state conventions and elections did not reveal any new main lines of development in radio and television techniques for presenting the news. There is plenty of room for doing better what is being done today—better commentators, better prepared to clarify political processes and personalities; more prompt and more accurate totalizing of results and reporting of decisions (let alone magic-brain predictions).

Reportage by television of the President's press conference attests to a growing range of application, and suggests possibilities for vigorous new growth in the experience and skill of television treatment of political matters. This is a salutary move, insofar as it makes a responsible representation of an important aspect of the presidency available for inspection to the people across the nation. Since the skillful initiatives of Franklin Roosevelt in dealing with the press, the President's press conference has taken a firmly-rooted place in our political procedures, as an institution by its very nature public, in which representatives of all press media can both seek and question official statements of executive views. The main operating issues stem from the requirement of editing, in which the White House reserves the right to eliminate from the televised version any part of the event. Thus the White House controls the presentation of the event to the public, judging, sometimes arbitrarily, what may or may not be included in the television version. This procedure finds main justification in the same argument that underlies the prohibition against quoting the President directly without express authorization. That is, the President's sometimes extemporaneous remarks should be considered against their possible impact on events either at home or abroad. Reasons of national interest, as well as of personal or party interest, may often justify this procedure. They are the same for the printed media as they are for radio or television; they are rarely wholly absent. At the same time, however, this procedure makes it possible for the White House staff to eliminate material putting the President or his party in an unfavorable light, which may or may not bear close relation to considerations of national rather than party interest.

Although television coverage of the President's press conference has no direct application to the problems of television coverage of the political conventions, experience so gained may help both parties and the broadcasters to handle edited coverage of the political events in a way that is responsive to the news, is impartial and objective, and in the public interest.

An even more pertinent and politically relevant development would be television coverage of congressional proceedings. This seems unlikely at the national level, given current congressional rulings. But there is experience at the state level, and abroad, and the possibility that Congress may open its proceedings to the camera at some time in the future.

Conversations with television directors active at the last conventions indicate a growing sense of professionalization, partly with respect to the technique of handling equipment but even more with respect to insight into the political process, and the results of the combination of increased efficiency in both departments. There is a growing sense of responsibility to seek out and report the essence of the event itself, subordinating the technical characteristics of the medium to this desired effect.

Will this growing sense of objectivity, this effort to record in the most conscientious way possible the essence of the convention event, be affected if other networks follow the CBS lead in adopting and expressing an editorial point of view, and if CBS develops it significantly? Will the impact of convention reportage via radio and television and the manner of treatment of the convention event be affected by such a development? There is no conclusive answer.

Present practice provides some clues to possible developments. It is generally agreed that station owners—particularly when they are publishers or politically prominent personages—already have political points of view, even though they may not express them via television or radio programs. It is commonly supposed that such preferences must be communicated to their employees in ways of varying subtlety, although the expression of such preferences is not sanctioned in any way by the official codes of conduct or policies for news presentation now in force in the various networks. It is also commonly known that newsmen and news editors have their political points of view and enjoy a large degree of freedom to express them overtly or by implication, no matter what the political preference of the employer. News analysts and announcers can do much in slanting their presentations by tone and mien, even if the cold words of the script are capable of quite other interpretation.

The current pace of development of an announced editorial point of view by the networks is slow. And the range of topics on which a network might assert its views is so far very limited. Will it be extended? This depends on the decisions of the makers of network editorial policy, but there are powerful reasons to conclude that this range will not be wide and may not include partisan politics at all. The gains of a network are nebulous and doubtful, if it takes a partisan stand. Its risks are large, involving its relations with its affiliated stations, with sponsors, with audiences, and with the government. Any network must live with a possibility of a change in administration. No network would wish lightly to prejudice its standing before the FCC or more generally before the government by taking a strong partisan position. Government can grant or withhold the one essential without which stations or networks cannot function—access to the electromagnetic spectrum.

The political preferences of owners of affiliated stations may not agree with those of the networks, and a built-in motive toward objectivity operates here just as it does in the case of the great press wire services, AP, UP, and INS. Multiple sponsorship may be necessary to meet the rising costs of television and may be made difficult or impossible if a sponsor desires neutrality or political agreement; and, just as many viewers now choose columnists and commentators and newspapers on the ground of political preference, they may set up political compatibility as a general ground for selecting network political programs.

Since the radio cases of the late 1930's, the only network editorial has had to do with a basic issue vital to the growth and effectiveness of radio-television news operations: access to legislative hearings. On August 26, 1954, Frank Stanton, President of CBS, delivered a CBS editorial defending the "right to be informed"; the nub of his plea was for an equal right for television to cover an event to which reporters with pencil and paper were admitted.[21] In this he went little further than the demand of the medium for access equal to that of other media to the convention proceedings of 1952. CBS championed the *right* to editorialize as early as 1948, but not until 1954 did the network exercise it. The FCC issued its views on the rights and duties of licensees to ensure fair and balanced presentation of programs dealing with controversial issues on June 2, 1949, in a release entitled "Editorializing by Broadcasting Licensees." This release reversed the

[21] "CBS Editorial," Frank Stanton. Pamphlet published by the Columbia Broadcasting System (no date). CBS invited Judge Harold R. Medina, of the United States Court of Appeals, to answer CBS arguments in equal time granted on Aug. 31, 1954.

earlier commission ban on editorializing, and stressed the public service responsibilities of the stations to provide balanced treatment of controversial issues. The commission reiterated these views in September 1954, as having particular applicability to current conditions, especially political reporting.[22]

On balance, it appears unlikely that the networks will move overtly toward partisan political positions. If they do, it is likely that they will clearly mark off their statements of preference from their news and news analysis functions, and will strongly underline the well-developed traditions of reporting both sides of an argument or contest to allay suspicions of unfair slanting of the news. But the suspicions of covert pressure are sure to increase. And if a network makes evident its preference for party or candidate before the conventions, there will be increased friction in arranging for television coverage of the convention of the opposing party and in dealing with opposing factions within the favored party. Hence it is likely that a network with a definite political position would defer any announcement of party preference until after the conventions, and might emphasize its support of a candidate rather than support of a party as such. But even this course becomes less tenable as it becomes more apparent that a political party and its candidate cannot effectively be disassociated from each other if either is to be held responsible for the conduct of the government.

It is interesting to speculate on the probable impact on national politics of the work of a genuinely national medium of daily news with a mature editorial point of view. We have national news magazines today, with strong editorial preferences, and national news services. But no newspaper reaches as far into the homes of all the people, and as

[22] FCC Public Notice (Sept. 8, 1954), p. 1.

promptly, as do national network television and radio. Possibly the expression of preference on these media, and its reflection in news treatment and analysis, would not affect politics in a manner appreciably different from the impact weekly news magazines already make. The responsiveness of the public to political events may be slow enough so the week-to-week impact is a close enough fit. But there is always the possibility, if a genuinely national daily news organ were in existence, that it could report and analyze a national event so as to affect the choice of a candidate or outcome of an election that will occur in less than a week's time. If the force of the event turned on its visual aspects, television would provide a novel force affecting electoral decisions. How different could this be from the present case, in which television already brings the news itself and its visual accompaniments immediately to the nation, and only the aspect of editorial viewpoint remains to be added? No one knows.

One possible gain to come from the taking of a mature editorial point of view by the networks would be an increase in the relative emphasis on the news and public service functions of the medium, over its current emphasis on entertainment and advertising.

CHAPTER V

Public Policy

AMONG the continuing issues of public policy that have emerged from the interrelationships of television and the nominating process are these:

1. Should the proceedings of each major party's national political convention be completely open to the press—including television coverage?

2. Should complete coverage of such proceedings be provided by the television industry as a public service obligation?

3. Should commercial sponsorship of the conventions be permitted, with paid advertising intermixed with reporting of the event?

4. Should television coverage stress news or entertainment values?

5. Should the networks make their political positions explicit while covering such political events as the conventions?

6. Should Section 315 of the Federal Communications Act be amended?

Convention Proceedings—Open or Closed?

The presumptive answer to the question whether the proceedings of the national convention of each major party should be completely open to the press is yes, in an open society such as ours. Any proceeding so fraught with importance for the life of the body politic should be open to public inspection. But this general question and this general answer call for qualification in important respects. First, what is included in the convention process as such? Is it confined to the formal meetings on the floor, or does it include the proceedings of the committees of the convention? And does coverage of the conventions call for coverage of the appurtenant meetings of the national committees of the two parties? The second main avenue of qualification arises from the question: What is included in the press?

The admission of the public to the formal meetings of the convention is a long-established practice, as is the practice of allowing access to all major press media. However, the question of access to the convention committee meetings and to the national committee meetings is not answered in the same way by both parties. Prior to 1952, the question of access of the press was settled on an *ad hoc* basis, and no particular furor was likely to be raised if these bodies decided to go into executive session. In that year the efforts of television to follow the news into meetings of the Republican National Committee dramatized the basic issue of access to these hearings. The networks had assumed their right to cover the committee hearings, and attempted to provide elaborate coverage that added to confusion and crowding in a room not adequately equipped to cope with the physical demands thus created. There were, moreover, strong reasons a majority of the committee did not wish to be subjected to, let alone take advantage of, the publicity television could provide.

At such proceedings as the credentials committee hearings, the story consists of three main elements: the hearings themselves (taking of testimony), the debate on the issues, and the voting. The Republicans have tended toward more secrecy in their proceedings than have the Democrats; the public has characteristically been excluded by the Republican National Committee from the voting and from substantial portions of its other proceedings. Hence uniform and traditional practice is no guide.

There should be little question of the right of the national committees, the convention committees, or the conventions themselves to decide whether their deliberations should be open or closed. Congress asserts and defends this right, as should any decision-making body that is charged with responsibility for important policy decisions in which there is a strong possibility that the public interest would be injured if all deliberations were held in public. A political party is in many respects like an army preparing for battle; it is too much to ask a general or a party leader to debate in public his strategy, his choice of subordinate commanders, or his order of battle. And much of the business of a party is compromise, the finding of inclusive solutions, and the resolution of differences in a manner that will respect the reputation and preserve the political effectiveness of important political groups and interests. A combination of privacy and of public debate seems indicated for the full discharge of these functions in a manner that is compatible with the right of the public to know what issues are being argued and what is being compromised.

The political party has an interest in achieving a proper although complicated synthesis of public and private action. A closed session is often a cause for distrust and suspicion, easily fanned by opposing factions and parties. No party can afford to gain a reputation for always making its basic decisions under the counter and for rigging public demonstrations to dramatize the results. And no party can afford to overlook the strength inherent in ability to conduct important debate and to arrive at solutions largely in public.

As a general principle, it can be recommended that the committees should hold their adversary hearings in public, and probably their final sessions of full committee debate and voting as well, with freedom to go into executive session from time to time—particularly on matters that will not go to the convention in any case. The public has a substantial right to know the major issues, the major arguments, and where the committee members stand on them. This does not mean that these points must all be reported immediately as they develop, but they can be made clear with full authority only if proceedings are so covered.

The question whether television should be excluded from any sessions to which other forms of the press are given access is a different issue and is presumptively clear: television should be allowed equal access, unless it can be shown that reportage via this medium tends to distort the proceedings themselves, or their outcome, in undesirable ways. The charge is often made[1] that television is an intruder; that it requires bulky equipment and high levels of lighting, thus adding to the inconvenience and discomfort of participants. The industry points out that television need not be obtrusive; that a camera need take up no more space than is required by two reporters; that levels of lighting are not a factor for black-and-white television, but only for color or for newsreel cameras; and that the machines are silent and the participants can well forget about them. There must be microphones to pick up the sound, but these can be used for both radio and television. And the requirements for broadcasting reporters and analysts can also be met jointly.

More important than the physical form of television is the influence that television coverage may have on the behavior of the participants. It is alleged to be difficult to maintain a judicial atmosphere so long as the committee members know they are on television—although television coverage undoubtedly increases the pressure to make the effort. And there is the ever-present possibility that awareness of the presence of the medium puts pressure on each committee member to make for his immediate constituents a record that may not always be compatible with a proper role as a member of a deliberative body. The temptation is undeniable. Experience to date is scant and provides no firm guide to future behavior or rules.[2] But so long as the pro-

---

[1] A charge made not only by parties or legislators but frequently by other press media in the course of intra-press competition.

[2] For a brief estimate of the impact of television on the behavior of lawmakers in legislative proceedings, see Paul Harkey, "Televising the Legislature in Oklahoma," *State Government* (October 1951). For the impact of radio, see Ralph Goldman, "Congress on the Air," *Public Opinion Quarterly*, Vol. 14, No. 4 (Winter 1950–51), pp. 744–52.

ceeding itself is public, there seems little reason to exclude television on the ground that its peculiar effects are especially distorting.

Is Complete Convention Coverage a Public Service Obligation?

Three aspects of the question, whether the television industry should give complete coverage as a public service obligation, require consideration. What is complete coverage? What is the nature of the public service obligation? Is the former required to discharge the latter?

Complete coverage could conceivably mean that the broadcasters should focus attention exclusively on floor proceedings from gavel to gavel on each day that the conventions are in session. But events within the hall are not independent of other closely related happenings; they may serve only to record decisions arrived at elsewhere, in committee meetings and caucuses. Thus a more politically meaningful and inclusive concept of full coverage calls for a running account of every happening related to the convention, either at the moment of occurrence or as shortly thereafter as possible, bringing the essential story of the choice of candidate and formulation of party policy. This may include coverage of the headquarters of each candidate; of each state delegation; of the convention committee meetings, as well as coverage of action on the floor or within the hall. It might reasonably include the preceding work of each national committee. The objective would be to broadcast as promptly as possible an exhaustive and coherent account of the actions and decisions of all participants in the convention that bear on the significant outcome of its work.

Such an ideal is an enormous undertaking, and may well remain only an ideal. On its surface, it would seem to call for live coverage, at least to provide the raw material at point of origin from which the editors of television can fashion what is transmitted on the air. But unprocessed live coverage cannot always suffice. The conventions are so organized that many actions can take place concurrently that bear vitally on the outcome. A now familiar case is the choice between action in convention committees and on the floor. Another possible case is that of a number of delegation caucuses concurrently deciding their position on a controversial point. It is thus not only possible but likely that a more meaningful and inclusive account could be constructed from film and tape, which would bring to the attention of the viewer the essentials of the story more completely and logically and in more digestible form than could a protracted eyewitness account of developments as they occur.

Live coverage has special advantages for certain types of material, most notably debates and votes on matters on which the convention must reach a decision. This material is often dramatic and always contains an element of hard news. News of this kind is conveyed more rapidly through live coverage than is possible in any other format, and it is also conveyed in greater depth. But set speeches, mimeographed and distributed in advance, are no more newsworthy in conventions than anywhere else, and no more necessarily entitled to live coverage. Availability of the speech may help the broadcaster to decide in advance whether he wants to cover it, and in what detail; it may be crucial in arranging for coverage of other aspects of the convention, such as committee meetings, in preference to the speech. For candidates and parties, full coverage is the best assurance of fair treatment, although the proceedings themselves are uneven in color and importance.

Not everything a convention does is equally newsworthy

or entitled to the same kind and amount of coverage. Convention behavior includes (1) opening routines and ceremonies at each session; (2) keynote speeches and other major addresses; (3) other political speeches scheduled mainly to fill time when business is not ready, usually because work is required in committee; (4) action on committee reports, including debates and votes; (5) speeches and demonstrations placing candidates in nomination; (6) the nominating roll calls and results; and (7) acceptance speeches and closing ceremonies.[3] It is impossible to make a firm decision in advance as to which of these types of action merits what type of coverage. Opening routines and ceremonies can be majestic or foolish, colorful or dull. Keynote speeches can be interminable harangues or sharp statements of public issues and positions on public policy. Action on committee reports can be of the most routine sort (in which case the

[3] Something of the problem the networks face in planning how to cover the conventions is revealed by an analysis of how the conventions spent their time in 1952. The following table shows that the Republicans devoted twice as much time to formalities, substantially more time to debate, about the same time to other speeches, less time to ovations, and a third as much time to voting as did the Democrats, whose voting procedures were much more cumbersome.

TIME BREAKDOWNS
1952 Conventions

	Formalities	Debate	Other Speeches	Ovations	Voting	Total
Minutes						
RNC	752 min.	341	746	224	240	2303 m (38h 23m)
DNC	483	224	903	369	773	2752 m (45h 52m)
Per Cent Time						
RNC	32.7	14.8	32.4	9.7	10.4	100.0
DNC	17.6	8.2	32.8	13.4	28.0	100.0

The pattern of future conventions need not follow these, which undoubtedly devoted more time to debate and voting on issues requiring convention action than most conventions. The broadcasters as well as the parties have to plan flexibly enough to cope with the unpredictable and the unknown, as well as the general structure of convention proceedings.

action is usually rapid, aside from reading the full text of each party platform), or can unfold with intense drama if further debate and voting reveals basic alignments on controversial issues. Nomination speeches can run a wide gamut. The nominating roll calls can proceed with complicated dreariness or hold great suspense as the major decision of the convention, and its manner of resolution, is worked out. Delegation splits, switches of support, and a dramatic denouement can come at any moment. And the acceptance speeches are now the opening salvo in the election campaign of the party.

These differences, with their possible variations, suggest that a combination of edited and live coverage will be most effective for most future conventions. Granted that editing will always play at least a part in such reportage, several important questions will have to be faced.

One such question is how to deal with the intangible problem of the possible differences in candidate or delegate behavior that might arise if the convention participant thought he was being televised—or that he was not, or wasn't sure. Live coverage suggests strongly to a subject that the nation is watching him. Would he behave differently if he thought that there was a good chance that any slip might be edited out, or that he might bring pressure to bear on the broadcaster to see that his cause or his person were put in a favorable light and that his opponents were not so well treated? Conscious of immediate nationwide reporting, a participant may behave well or ill; he may forget himself and the fact that he is being televised. Generalization is impossible.

Preparation of an edited account puts great responsibility and pressure on the newscasters, calling for the maximum of insight, maturity, and impartiality, and offering opportunities both for public service or less laudable ends. But editing must always go on, even with live coverage, as long as six to twenty cameras are running with pictures on monitoring receivers in the editorial center for pooled coverage and at the network centers. The opportunities for public service are enormous, as a good edited account could well conserve the public's time, bring the account at times and places when most of the public could watch it, and include the most relevant parts of concurrent events.

What is the public service obligation of the networks? The Communications Act requires licensees to serve the public interest, convenience, and necessity. And the regulations and decisions of the Federal Communications Commission put them under obligation to ensure fair and balanced presentation of programs relating to important public issues of a controversial nature, including political broadcasts. These obligations are necessarily general.

Should there be a specific requirement that the broadcasters cover the conventions fully as a necessary act to discharge this general obligation? No, for at least two reasons. First, convention broadcasting is not the only form of public service that broadcasters should perform. Although conventions are traditionally regarded as a dominant special event while they occur, and the broadcasters have always cleared time to carry them, they need not always have pride of place against other events. The second reason is that the conventions themselves need not always remain an important facet of our political life. If we adopted national presidential primaries, portions of the convention procedure might turn into something no more meaningful or dramatic than the electoral college. And in any event, when the nomination is uncontested and the act is only a *pro forma* confirmation of the existing party leadership—as it has been in more than twenty of the sixty-one major party nominations since 1831 —the conventions inevitably lose much of their special drama and significance. So any continuing formal obligation to report all national party conventions as a public service would be unwarranted.

Taking the most probable assumption, that the conventions will remain a vital part of our political processes for a considerable time to come, it still seems clear that full, live coverage is not necessary to an adequate discharge of the public service obligations of the networks. A combination of editing and live coverage seems to offer the most likely prospect of bringing the essence of the event to the television audience. And the interest of the broadcasting industry in covering an important political event remains as sufficient guarantee that the major conventions will be given much fuller treatment than most other special events.

Should the Conventions Be Commercially Sponsored?

The issue whether broadcasting coverage of the conventions should be commercially sponsored was put sharply in preparations for the 1952 campaign. Previously in the experience both of radio and television, such coverage had not been sponsored by any advertisers, but had been carried by the broadcasters as a public service. With the advent of full-fledged television, however, it was apparent that the costs of coverage would go up, and the networks sought to offset them. After some negotiations with the national committees, which did not apparently turn much on the propriety of sponsorship but rather on sharing the benefits and the costs, the 1952 conventions were commercially sponsored both as to radio and television.

It now appears that future conventions will also be commercially sponsored.[4] This outcome, even if unchallenged,

[4] As of Dec. 1, 1955, only one network (CBS) had made firm arrangements for sponsorship of convention, campaign, and election returns coverage for 1956. The

leaves open one important latent question of principle, and several questions of detail that are of continuing interest.

The continuing latent issue turns on the very nature of sponsorship itself: What is the relation of the sponsor to the event covered? In broadcasting argot, a sponsor is simply a person, real or artificial, who pays for a block of time over one or more stations, and in addition pays for the cost of programing that amount of time. In return he receives the right to advertise his goods or services in a manner consistent with network agreements, industry standards, and the conscience and good taste of American advertising. In the common commercial application of sponsorship, there is usually no implication that the advertiser stands as a social sponsor of the event or of the program for which he pays. (Consider the case of college football games.) But the question of the control that a sponsor may exercise over the content of a broadcast often presents difficulties, which are recognized in the policies and practices of the networks. Thus the networks or individual stations commonly take full responsibility for underwriting news services, and do not allow such services to be "sponsored" in any way in which the sponsor could affect the content of the news program. But news

---

others expected sponsors to be forthcoming. The CBS arrangement with the Westinghouse Electric Corporation, announced July 27, 1955, called for an outlay of $5 million by the sponsor for both radio and television coverage, including special programs the day before the opening of the Democratic and Republican conventions, broadcasts direct from the conventions, a nine-week series of debates on election issues, and broadcasts of returns on election night. Factors underlying the increased subvention ($5 million for 1956 against $3 million for 1952) were the increase in sets (17.6 million in 1952, 40 million estimated for 1956) and the increased cost of providing duplicate facilities for Chicago and for San Francisco. The conventions were expected to be shorter, however.

In stating the estimate of Westinghouse of the effects of television and radio coverage, President Gwilym A. Price said: "Many political observers believe that the enormous vote which turned out in the last Presidential election . . . was in part a result of the way in which television carried the conventions and the campaign right into the living rooms of America. Westinghouse hopes that this next campaign will repeat that heartening result." Val Adams, " '56 Coverage Set by Westinghouse," *New York Times* (July 28, 1955), p. 47.

analysis and news commentary are not always so treated. Most of the commentators today are sponsored, and the name of the product is placed in close proximity to the news content of the show, sometimes by the news analyst himself. The extent of possible control is sometimes hinted at by the fact that reputable and popular network political reporters and analysts have been taken off the air because a sponsor had withdrawn his support of the show, and no new sponsor could be found. One of the networks in particular made it a point of policy to bring news analysis and commentary on a sustaining basis; such practice of course raises only the question of the relations of the network to the commentator.

But in the field of political television, the question, otherwise chiefly one of taste, becomes acute if the extent and nature of coverage turns on the presence or absence of commercial sponsorship. The networks argued powerfully in 1952 that sponsorship of their convention broadcasting was justified because with the additional resources they could do a more complete job of news coverage and analysis. Such a situation contains the obvious possibility that a network might give some thought to planning news coverage in such a way as to make the convention a more sponsorable event. At worst, this could be unfortunate. At best, a main condition of sponsorability would call for a complete hands-off attitude on the part of the sponsor. The most likely condition is, however, that the demands of a sponsor for personal or company neutrality would force him into an adequately neutral pose.

When the event is a political convention, and one of the institutional values to be derived from it is a reputation for public service, which comes from that very association of public event and private company, the connotations of sponsorship go beyond the question of a sponsor's relations to the news treatment of the political event. These further aspects were recognized by both parties and by the networks in their negotiations over sponsorship of the 1952 conventions, and were reflected in those provisions of the resulting agreement that called for a disclaimer made at the beginning and end of each broadcast period. The purpose of this disclaimer was to make perfectly clear that the client is sponsoring the coverage of the event by the network, and that sponsorship does not imply in any manner an endorsement of the political party by the sponsor or of the product of the sponsor by the political party. It was also provided that commercial announcements should be so written, programed, and delivered that they would be clearly separated from convention proceedings, political parties, issues, and personalities. A further provision in the interest of separation was that no commercial announcements might be made from the floor of the convention.

No prominent flare-up after the 1952 conventions suggested that the American people had been hoodwinked on the relation between the sponsor, the networks, and the convention. Yet the possibility of misunderstanding persists because of the intimacy of the intermixture of convention reporting and the interspersed commercials.

Gilbert Seldes has proposed that the answer to the problem is to have the networks bring the convention as a public service, with commercial messages at appropriate intervals. "Sponsorship associates a product with the content of the broadcast; commercial spots do nothing of the sort; in the first, the sponsor is, as his name implies, responsible; in the second, the network is." [5] Seldes recognizes the possibility that the audience will not see the difference and will still think the advertiser is entitled to gratitude for "bringing"

[5] Gilbert Seldes, "Politics—Televised and Sponsored," *Saturday Review of Literature* (Mar. 15, 1952).

the convention, but asserts the difference is clear and decisive. And the procedure insisted on by the party committees is certainly preferable to other alternatives, in which the advertiser provides straight sponsorship and the announcer states that——company gives you the national convention, or the——company presents the next President of the United States, or the sponsor brings the political event "as a public service."

Seldes undoubtedly has something of a point, even though it would be difficult to prove that commercial spots do not associate a product or a company with the content of a broadcast. Certainly most thoughtful citizens would deem it offensive if their daily newspaper were "sponsored" by Westinghouse or Philco or Admiral during each of the five or six days while a national party convention is in progress. The networks have not proved that it is impossible to cover the conventions adequately as a part of their normal news and special events service without bringing the sponsors into closer relationship to the coverage than any reputable newspaper would tolerate for its news and editorial columns. So long as the issue remains in any way open, moreover, the burden of proof for so compromising a relationship must inevitably remain on the networks and on the stations that regularly come up for the renewal of their licenses. Even if it is necessary that one advertiser be given a monopoly of the commercial broadcasts of a network in conjunction with a convention, why is it necessary to say, at repeated intervals (as required by FCC regulations), that the advertiser is *sponsoring* the network coverage of the event? In fact, it is when the sponsor is a single advertiser rather than several that the whole sponsorship relation becomes most questionable.

Other related questions are these: Who is an appropriate sponsor? What financial interests do the parties have in convention sponsorship? Do the party committees have a proper claim for any portion of the sponsorship fees? Should any legal standards or controls be set up to regulate sponsorship of these events? Should the sponsor have any control over the broadcasts? And should sponsors be allowed to bring one convention, but not the other?

The question who is an appropriate sponsor poses differing issues to differing participants in political broadcasting. The parties are interested in seeing that the sponsor or his product will not provide unfortunate associations—hence agreements that sponsors associated with perfumery and colonic regularity or emergency, along with products activating moralistic scruples such as liquor, would not be permitted. The networks are interested in sponsors wealthy enough to contribute substantially to the costs of coverage, and possibly to provide a net cash return, as well as an appropriate presentation of the total event. The public is interested in seeing a full and detailed treatment of the convention, with a minimum of interruption for station identification or for sponsors' messages.

The political parties have a continuing proprietary interest in the appearance of the conventions as party functions, in no way associated with the sponsor as such, and in no way subservient to the interest of the sponsor. This runs close to the interest of the sponsor in associating himself with public service and an important political function. It is doubtful whether any formal control could effectively be devised to separate the two, or whether under current conditions any is needed. The preservation of mutual interests on the part of the parties and the sponsors can be counted on to adjust differences.

The financial interest of the parties in convention sponsorship has not been deeply probed. The issue of how to divide the profits from sponsor contributions to the networks was touched in 1951–52, but chiefly in connection with the question who would pay for the special installation costs of television. In the event, there were no visible direct net profits in the year 1952. But there could be, particularly if the networks were to adopt a plan of sharply edited coverage; did not make heavy expenditures for special equipment or unusual installations; and arranged their commercial contracts so as to keep pre-emption costs to a minimum. (These are paid by the sponsor in any event, but if pre-emption costs are low, the networks might be able to drive up the price of convention sponsorship to cover more than the time and installation costs.) If the networks seemed to be in a position to make a profit from political coverage, the parties might be able to drive bargains along two lines. They might charge the networks a fee for the right to televise the conventions. Or they might bargain for a good quota of public service time during the campaigns.

What if the sponsor were an individual? There are such, wealthy enough to pay a multi-million dollar bill. The implications are intriguing, but the possibility of the event is so far-fetched as to rule out any worth-while speculation on this point.

The question of legal standards and controls over sponsorship has not been explored; the experience of only one set of conventions hardly provides adequate grounds to indicate whether any are in the public interest.

To ask the question whether sponsors should have any control over convention proceedings is to answer it. Of course not. It would be neither in the interest of the sponsor nor of the party. But this does not rule out a host of efforts by the various interested actors in the total scene—including sponsors and their advertising agencies—to affect these proceedings. There are enough of them, and with enough divergence of interest, to keep the event from being unduly stage-managed.

Finally, should sponsors be free to sponsor one convention but not the other? Here again, the interest of the sponsor seems to rule this question out as a practical issue. If a single sponsor took only one convention, he would run grave risk of identifying himself with a single party. But there is the possibility that sponsorship could be widely shared, and a different group might underwrite each convention. Mutual's radio broadcasting of the conventions of 1952 was on a "co-operative" basis. NBC is vigorously pursuing the possibilities of joint commercial sponsorship of its "spectaculars" and its "participating programs," "Today," "Home," and "Tonight." Both NBC and CBS are working out devices for multiplying sponsors for these and other shows—possibly in anticipation of trends in the marketing patterns of television, which reveal increasing stress on local outlets and local service. Under such systems, the network would arrange for appropriate insertions of "billboard items" by a variety of contributing sponsors, in both conventions. The "magazine concept" could be very easily applied to the electoral process as a whole, and multiple sponsors obtained for pre-convention, convention, campaign, and election-night coverage.

Whatever the motive, the trend in television is toward multiple sponsorship. Multiple sponsorship of conventions, already here in practice in mild form, may do something to soften issues that seem much more sharp when single sponsorship is under contemplation by each major network. Governmental control does not seem necessary.

Should Network Editors Stress News or Entertainment?

In view of the well-established emphasis of television on entertainment, the possibility exists that it will stress entertainment values to an inordinate degree, presenting the conventions as entertainment rather than a serious event that is covered for the instruction of the politically curious. That such a possibility exists is undeniable. But it is remote, and there are strong checks against it. In the first place, those responsible for critical decisions about convention coverage do not come from sectors of the industry that are primarily concerned with entertainment. They are, on the contrary, specialists in reporting and analyzing news and public affairs. They are sustained by their professional pride and skills, and protected by the continuing interest of the medium in giving public service functions considerable prominence.

As television grows and matures, there are grounds for hope that more emphasis will be placed on its news functions, not only as a means of providing a minimum of public service, but as a basic method of earning a living. Hence sponsorship of convention television gains justification insofar as it offers the opportunity to make money by providing an outstanding news service, and thus pull the emphasis of television in a desirable direction.

Even if it were clear that almost exclusive stress should be placed on news and commentary, there is a case for judicious inclusion of entertainment aspects. Entertainment can help build audiences and win sustained attention to what, after all, is a fairly complicated process. Entertainment, moreover, is sometimes inescapable. It is part of the news. The behavior of the Puerto Rican delegation to the Republican convention in 1952 certainly demonstrates how unwitting but delicious entertainment may emerge from the most factual and straightforward news coverage.

A further question relating to the manner of news treatment of the conventions is this: Should the television reporters provide the absolute minimum of comment, in the belief that camera action and the actual sound track picked up from the official proceedings will give the viewer an adequate comprehension of what is going on? Or should the newscasters and analysts provide considerable running comment and explanation, to the end that the wider significance of each development is made clear as it occurs? The broadcasters vacillated between these poles during the 1952 conventions, partly because they felt they had not let the event come through with sufficient clarity in Philadelphia in 1948. In 1952 they hesitated to interrupt speakers even to identify them, and usually did this by visual means without interrupting the sound track. But it is possible that they should do more than they did to keep complicated parliamentary situations clear, and to assess the factional or regional significance of committee or convention votes as they are recorded. Growing political sophistication—to which television can contribute—might reduce the need for such comment. But we have not yet come as a nation to the point where we can look at a convention as expertly as we can observe baseball. So comment, impartial but pungent, remains a requirement for 1956 and beyond.

Should the Networks State Their Political Preferences?

The issue whether networks and stations should make their political preferences explicit while they are reporting political conventions or campaigns, lies barely beneath the surface. The standard practice of broadcasting has been to preserve a formal neutrality, and the network newscasters have achieved a high standard of objectivity. Yet in 1952 many observers thought that the owners and top management of the networks, if not the majority of broadcasting stations, were back of Eisenhower. It was equally apparent that many newscasters and analysts had their preferences, too, although their support for the candidates was more evenly divided. This gave rise to an undercurrent of uneasiness at least in intellectual circles, even though there was no widespread evidence that the public thought its news was being unduly colored by the sympathies of owners or of news staffs.

The general principle of public policy governing communications in our society calls for a communicator to make his interests, his sponsors, and his preferences, if any, clearly known, so the recipient of his communications can judge for himself the credibility and the bias of what is communicated. Moreover, it is difficult for the public to imagine that owners and news staffs do not have their preferences. In the face of this, is it possible for broadcasters to preserve full faith and credit in the absence of a statement of political preference?

Comparison with newspaper practice may throw additional light on this question. Newspapers carry a long tradition of intimate mutual relations with politics and are nevertheless tending toward greater objectivity and impartiality in their news reporting, particularly when judged against the political reporting of a century ago.[6] Newspapers play a responsible part in our political life, supporting candidates and taking sides on issues while maintaining news services judged reasonably full and accurate, and impartial at least in the sense of giving some space to both sides of a controversy. The wire services have special reason to maintain objectivity, as noted above.

If newspapers can support this dual role, why not the networks? The main element of newspaper practice underlying success in this role is clear separation between the editorial page and its news activities—a separation equally available to television, by ordinary devices of time management and labeling of the intent of each broadcast. The juxtaposition of advertising to news columns is just as close as a sponsor's

---

[6] See Frank Luther Mott, *American Journalism* (1940).

announcement or sales effort to the content of a telecast. If the networks in fact do have preferences, is it not more honest to say so, and let the viewer judge news analysis, commentary, and reporting in the light of the stated preference? And from the standpoint of networks and stations, is it not worth while to let the viewer judge whether the news commentator agrees with his boss—and to take heart from the frequent instances in which he does not?

The other side of the picture shows the values to be found in a reinforcement of the traditional emphasis of the broadcaster on official neutrality. Even if not fully susceptible of achievement, high standards of neutrality, objectivity, and impartiality in reporting play a powerful role. The consequences have not yet been illuminated by research findings in their present form, although some subjects for such research are already available in the United Nations news broadcasts, in which neutrality is enforced by the structure and continuing interests of the organization itself. The ancient vacillation between partisan and neutral reporting will undoubtedly continue, as excesses in partisanship make cool neutrality welcome, and the dreariness of neutrality opens the way for the sprightliness and color of partisanship.

Achievement of a true neutrality may be somewhat difficult in American broadcasting in view of the extent to which broadcasting outlets are owned by newspaper publishers—the single most numerous category of owners. Most of these publishers are politically active and vocal, making their preferences for candidates and parties clearly known in their newspapers. How, then, can an appearance of broadcasting neutrality be maintained in the face of the position of the newspaper that owns the station?

Movement toward a clear statement of editorial position may be hampered by the feeling on the part of station owners that their position before the FCC will be jeopardized if they play a clear partisan role. The interests of station owners continue, no matter what political party is in power, or what political currents dominate the thinking of the regulatory agency. It is a safer policy to establish a forum, and to hold debate in which controversial issues are argued out or dissected by guests rather than by station employees.

If there were a strong desire on the part of the networks to move toward statements of editorial position, the question arises: Who will be first penguin in the water? CBS has wet a wing, but has not yet really tempted the sharks. CBS owns a few stations,[7] but it is primarily a provider of programs to affiliated stations. And it is the stations that bear responsibility for discharging the terms of their licenses. Even if a network did take the plunge, it might find itself talking only over its owned-and-operated outlets. Other stations might not care to risk carriage of network-originated news and commentary, if they thought it was politically suspect (*i.e.*, liable to jeopardize their neutrality). However, the stations are concerned that the public should know the preferences of the networks responsible for originating much of the most important news services—unless the networks can in fact achieve neutrality.

The issue today is moot. Public policy counsels statement of preferences where they exist, as a step required for full public understanding of what is communicated. The public interest may benefit greatly from further development toward objective and impartial news services, supplemented by an effective forum in which protagonists of various points of view can illuminate all important aspects of controversial issues, including the issues involved in the choice of party nominees and candidates.

[7] Four in mid-1955, with actions to get more pending before the FCC. Ownership by one individual or corporation of a maximum of 7 television stations (no more than 5 VHF) is permitted under the FCC multiple-ownership rule.

Should Section 315 of the Federal Communications Act Be Amended?

Section 315 of the Federal Communications Act provides that holders of broadcasting licenses shall give equal access to all bona fide candidates for political office, or nomination therefor; and it prohibits censorship of the utterances of any such candidates. The standard of equal treatment is reasonably well met today, although the accidents of time and circumstance, the pocketbooks of the candidates and the parties, and the characteristics of radio and television broadcasting make it Utopian to think that all candidates and parties can have exactly equal opportunities to express their political pleas. But the achievement of full access falls well short of ideal, and the definition of candidates and the prohibition of station censorship seem to be working against it.

In their testimony before the Senate Subcommittee on Privileges and Elections, the networks explained clearly how the requirement of equal access to candidates operates to reduce access to the medium. This testimony goes beyond the point of candidate's access to show how the requirement prevents forms of political discourse that would be of great public interest and value, such as debates between the nominees of the two major parties. In the words of Richard S. Salant, "The fact unquestionably is that Section 315 keeps us from covering political campaigns, and presenting candidates, as extensively and as intelligently as we would otherwise do."[8]

Much but not all of the networks' difficulties arising out of Section 315 relate to campaigning *after* the nominations. Section 315 includes candidates *for the nominations;* and it re-

---

[8] See the testimony of Richard S. Salant, Executive Vice President, CBS, before the Senate Subcommittee on Privileges and Elections, April 1955 (CBS mimeo., no date), p. 10.

quires a network presenting the major candidates on one of its sustaining pre-convention programs to open its facilities to all other candidates for the nomination whether or not they have anything important to say or represent any substantial body of persons or opinion. FCC decisions in the Schneider case (see above, p. 25) and in other cases,[9] press the networks to reduce to a minimum the appearances of people who are avowed candidates for the nomination. Salant concluded: "Section 315 and Mr. Schneider make us very doubtful that our pre-convention coverage in 1956 can be nearly as complete as it was in 1952."[10]

The issue of prohibition of censorship of the utterance of any candidate seems simple on its face. Stations should obviously not interfere with the political statements of candidates. However, in practice it is more difficult. The prohibition is clear and sweeping, insofar as it concerns the freedom of candidates to say exactly what they please. The FCC has decided that the candidate need not stick to political issues, but can say anything he deems best.[11] Even if he were to call for revolution, the station could do nothing about it in advance, and might be held jointly liable for abetting a criminal utterance. Stations as a matter of practice can ask for copies of candidates' speeches in advance, and try to persuade them against any utterances that they feel would put the network or the station in an improper or false position;

[9] The FCC has decided that the appearance of a candidate on such a show as "Pick the Winner" requires an offer of substantially equal opportunity to other candidates for the same office. This time need not be on the same show, but the obligation is not discharged by providing an equivalent amount and class of time. The audience as affected by the first candidate's appearance must be considered. The FCC regards the parties as responsible for initial efforts toward an agreeable solution. See letter of FCC to CBS, Oct. 31, 1952, requiring the offer to the vice-presidential candidate of the Socialist Workers party opportunity to use CBS facilities equal to that enjoyed by Senator Sparkman. The FCC has also decided that reports of senators to their people constitute a use of facilities within the meaning of Section 315 if the senator is a legally qualified candidate for office. Declarative ruling of the FCC, May 15, 1952, in the matter of Radio Station KNGS, Hanford, California.

[10] Testimony of Richard S. Salant, April 1955 (CBS mimeo., no date), p. 12.

[11] See FCC Public Notice of Sept. 8, 1954, p. 4, which cites the FCC ruling in the case of WMCA, Inc. (7 R.R. 1132).

but they cannot insist on seeing the speech in advance, let alone make any deletions or changes without the speaker's consent.

Better solutions of the issues are not easily found. If the networks and stations were given more freedom under the law or its interpretation to determine who is a substantial candidate in an open nominating contest, enormous power would be granted to them. While television is not indispensable to political success, it has unique characteristics that make it especially valuable to the political late-comer. The public is interested in a wide choice among competent candidates, and the accidents or designs of network or station policy should not be allowed unduly to hamper that range of selection.

The broadcasters could now, under the law, reduce drastically the amount of public service time granted to candidates for nomination. They are already hinting that they must do so, and have indicated their willingness to sell time to political office-seekers in the pre-convention period. By closing their public service time to avowed candidates for the nomination, networks or stations could press potential candidates toward withholding declarations of candidacy until the last possible moment, in order to preserve their chances of getting on television as invited guests. This would further reduce the importance of the existing presidential primaries in which candidacies must be avowed or not disavowed in order to participate effectively, as in New Hampshire and several other states. The stations would still retain their present great power to decide who is to be selected to appear on various occasions when candidacies have not yet become overt. It would give an advantage to potential candidates already in some office—governors or congressmen—who have access to television by virtue of their public position.

There appear to be four courses of action with respect to

the equal-access provisions of Section 315: (1) leave them alone; (2) remove them from the law, and leave complete discretion with licensees to govern access of candidates to the air; (3) have the government purchase or pre-empt time for political broadcasting; (4) revise the standard in the act.

As to the first course, it now appears that the networks and stations are serious about limiting public service political time in the pre-convention period, and view with great misgivings the problem of political broadcasting, even on a paid or news-show basis, in the campaign period. To leave the section untouched is to risk real diminution of the usefulness of television as a medium of political communication.

To remove all standards governing equal access from the law, leaving the judgment to the licensees as to who can use the potentialities of television and when, seems to delegate excessive political power and responsibility to the networks and stations. The networks and stations are not requesting it, and no one has seriously suggested this course of action.

To have the government purchase or pre-empt a good block of political time, under the legal principle that access to the electromagnetic spectrum is a privilege granted by government and revocable by it, is a proposal that has had a good many recent proponents. But if the government were to buy time from the networks and make it available to all comers, there would be a long series of headaches or worse in sorting out political time among the various applicants. If the government were to force the networks to give up enough time to accommodate everybody, this would amount to a taking of property (not the access to the spectrum, but the right to sell time over broadcasting stations). Such a taking might be justified on the ground that it is for a legitimate public purpose, but the facts might not bear it out. In the case of candidates toward the fringe of seriousness and political stature, there might be no public gain. And the public stands

to suffer from an overdose of political television and depriva-
tion of substantial quantities of its accustomed television
programing. Underlying both procedures would be the question whether it is better to have government or private decisions as to who shall have access to one communications
medium. The industry has already made the point that it is
unfair for the government to force television to give up
valuable air time for political broadcasting, when similar
deprivations are not required from other media. Possibly
more important are those issues that revolve on the question
of the propriety of allowing a government agency to make
vital decisions concerning the freedom of competing political
organizations to conduct campaigns and discuss issues.

The final course is to revise the standard in the act, so as
to improve the chances of full political use of television while
avoiding some of the difficulties and dangers of the other
courses. Two steps under this course of action seem worthy
of public discussion. As a first step, amend the Communications Act so as to define a *major party* and to make the equal-
time provision apply only to candidates of such parties, or
their authorized representatives, and leave to the discretion
of stations decisions on how far their general responsibilities for giving balanced treatment to controversial issues
require them to give time to other political parties.[12] The
second step would be to amend the act further to define a
leading candidate, and to restrict the benefits of the equal-time
provision to leading candidates of major parties in the case of
pre-nomination campaigns. Since these two steps are separa-
ble and involve somewhat different issues of administration,
they are discussed separately.

The problem of defining a major party has been dealt with
often, to all intents and purposes, by state legislation in con-

[12] See editorial, *Washington Post and Times-Herald* (June 27, 1955), p. 18; and
letter from Frank Stanton, President, CBS, in the same issue.

nection with the admission of parties to the primary election machinery of the states. And the pending Douglas-Bennett Bill proposes a federal criterion for a national party.[13] The important point is to require a certain minimum of electoral support distributed over several states.

A proposal to define major parties and to make the equal-time provision run to them would open the way to a better balanced and more varied use of television time for political purposes during the campaign itself. If the broadcasters had to assure equal treatment only for four candidates—two for President and two for Vice President—at the national level, they might find it advisable to give public service time more generously after the nominations.[14] They might also find it possible to produce forms of political discussion that are now too risky to attempt. The parties might bargain with the broadcasters for a trade of the valuable property of their convention against a definite allotment of time for political purposes during the campaign.[15] And the requirement of equal

[13] See Paul T. David, Malcolm Moos, Ralph M. Goldman, *Presidential Nominating Politics in 1952*, Vol. I (1954), p. 217. The criterion for a party proposed there is that the organization shall have polled at least 10 million votes in the past presidential election. The Democratic and Republican parties are the only political parties that have ever met this criterion in the United States.

[14] Anticipating a possible change in Section 315, President Stanton of CBS announced on May 23, 1955, that CBS and its affiliated television stations would offer free network time to the presidential candidates of the two major parties in 1956 for a series of "electronic 'Lincoln-Douglas' debates." In the press release making the offer, Dr. Stanton pointed out that the network was not asking for freedom to pick and choose in carrying ordinary campaign speeches, whether made in the course of political rallies or delivered in the studios. Nor would CBS modify its policy of not granting free time once the campaign has begun. To permit the debate between the candidates of the two major parties, Dr. Stanton suggested that Section 315 be amended by adding the following provision: "Appearance by a legally qualified candidate on any news, news interview, panel discussion, debate or similar type program where the format and production of the program and the participants therein are determined by the broadcasting station, or by the network in the case of a network program, shall not be deemed to be use of a broadcasting station within the meaning of this subsection."

[15] The suggestion that the parties might bargain with the networks for an exchange of the right to cover the conventions by television for a good share of public service time during the campaign, has its pitfalls. The networks might be able to play the parties off against each other, and restrict both convention coverage and post-conven-

treatment would work toward an equitable balance of the contribution of television to the campaigns of both parties, and reduce the advantages now possible to whichever party has the deeper pocketbook or the more astute time-buyers.

This proposal is open to the objection that it discriminates unjustly against new or minor political parties, and makes it more difficult for new political constellations to take form. The force of this objection is reduced by the observation that the formation of new political parties is probably no longer a feasible way to shift our basic political arrangements. New political forces will mainly make themselves felt within the framework of the existing major parties, or will appear as results of the fission of one or the other of them. Even if this argument is not wholly sound, it would nevertheless be possible so to design a redrafted Section 315 as to protect the interest of any third party that could amass a certain minimum of political support—poll, say, 1,000,000 votes in a national election with at least 100,000 in each of five or more states; or produce a petition for recognition as a major party signed by a comparable number of voters.

The foregoing remedy would help the ills of political broadcasting during the campaign period, but would not help in the pre-convention period. So far, neither the industry nor political candidates have come up with any solutions that seem both politically just and administratively workable for the earlier and longer period. Hence the second step we propose may merit serious consideration.

This step requires a definition of "leading candidates" as well as of "major parties." The problem of defining a leading *candidate* has not been attempted, as has the definition of

---

tion time, if one or both conventions did not appear to be particularly newsworthy in any campaign. With increasing costs of, and commercial demand for television time, the networks are in an increasingly strong bargaining position that may not be matched by that of the parties.

"party," but is susceptible of solution. A statutory definition substantially as follows might suffice: "A leading candidate for a party nomination shall be deemed to be any candidate who is able, on demand, to adduce substantial evidence of his probable ability to secure at least 15 per cent of the vote on the first ballot of the party convention or primary in which the party nomination will be made." Such a criterion could easily be applied in the first instance by networks or stations. In cases of controversy in which the licensee did not want to stretch its interpretation of the facts, and the prospective candidate was determined to assert his right to air time, the matter could be taken to the Federal Communications Commission or to the courts. Evidence of meeting the standard could come from at least four sources: (1) reputable polling surveys, by Gallup or others; (2) extent of announced support by political leaders; (3) results in state primaries; and (4) expert opinion, based on these and other factors.

The level of 15 per cent is not sacrosanct; it could be put up or down. But to drop the level to 10 per cent might permit a favorite son from one of the most populous states to qualify simply on the basis of support in a single state. To raise it to 20 per cent would be to put it unnecessarily high. The experience of 1952 shows that a 15 per cent level would have restricted the equality requirement to the real leading candidates. In the Republican convention, only Taft and Eisenhower polled as much as 10 per cent at any time. In the Democratic convention, Kefauver, Russell, and Stevenson each polled over 20 per cent; Harriman barely 10 per cent; and no other candidate over 6 per cent. The only serious contender who would have been excluded was Stevenson, and this on the ground that he refused to be a candidate in the pre-convention period.

The kinds of candidates who would be omitted by such criteria would be frivolous candidates, favorite sons without much following outside their own states, and candidates of minor parties. And they would not be excluded from the air. On the contrary, their chances of access might actually be increased. If they proved themselves really noteworthy because of their ideas or their personalities, the networks would want to put them on, and would not be inhibited from doing so by the present rigid equality provisions.

Section 315 could advantageously be redrawn to assure equal treatment to the candidates for President and Vice President of major parties during the campaign period. In addition, the act might well be further redrawn to restrict the legal requirement of equal time to the leading candidates of major parties during pre-nomination campaigns for these offices.[16] The result should be a more intensive and searching presentation of politics on television, featuring confrontations between the major contenders. A further result might be a more varied diet, as networks or stations could present a variety of political candidates without exposing themselves to undue demands on their schedules, or having to inject excessive doses of possibly trivial political personalities or ideas into their programs. More important, such redrafting would reduce the risk that licensees will cut their political broadcasting to the absolute minimum in self-protection. The FCC should be alert, however, to see that licensees are not lax in carrying out their public service obligations.

Should the censorship provisions of Section 315 be redrawn? This question deals with a situation in which attempts at cure might be worse than the disease. The networks and stations are not too badly off now, and the candidates are in a strong position (if they can get air time at all). No Communists have seized the opportunity to promote rev-

---

[16] While the present suggestion is restricted to national offices, it might lead to valuable experience that would in turn open up similar possibilities for political television in state and in local campaigns.

olution via television. The changes in their status worked
by the Communist Control Act of 1954 have not been fully
determined, but the act diminishes danger. Many stations,
acting within the temper of the times, already refuse time to
Communists or other persons suspected of Communist
affiliations. Most candidates are grateful enough for access to
television to be willing to work intelligently and co-opera-
tively with it, opening themselves up to the kind of advice
which offers *de facto* protection to the broadcaster against
suits for libel or for abetting criminal utterance.

Given these mitigating circumstances, it would seem that
the threat of political crisis would have to deepen a good deal
further before tighter censorship is timely. And if it does
come, it is likely that closer controls over candidates will be
more important than controls over stations.[17] It does seem,
however, given continuation of our relative domestic tran-
quillity, that if stations are prohibited from censoring the
utterances of candidates, or even requiring that they stick
to a theme related to their candidacy, the stations should be
relieved by federal law (as they are in many states) of liabil-
ity arising out of such utterances.[18]

[17] This would be true in conditions of social tension short of a point where a single
treasonable utterance over a broadcasting station could suffice to trigger revolution.

[18] The FCC has supported this position in the past in its comments to Congress on
proposed legislation, and the commission has discussed its intricacies in the Port
Huron decision (12 FCC 1069). *Editor and Publisher* has taken the opposite position
that there should be no discrimination between news media, and therefore broadcasters should be given both the power to censor political utterances, and clear responsibility for any libelous material uttered over their facilities. (See editorial,
July 12, 1952, p. 40.)

CHAPTER VI

The Future Political Importance of Television

I T IS now in order to cast up a tentative estimate of the relations of television to politics—the nominating process in particular—and to gauge roughly the impact of this new medium.

Television will affect candidates, conventions, and campaigning. It will affect the selection and prospects of candidates both before and during the conventions. It will affect the location, the timing, the procedure, and the behavior of nominating conventions. It will send the chosen nominee of each convention into the subsequent campaign with much of his political personality established and his public image fashioned for the voter. Television has already changed the timing and techniques of campaigning, as demonstrated by practice in 1952 and 1954, and by action already taken and in prospect for 1956 and beyond.

Television tactics will change somewhat, as technical developments in the industry offer new and more inclusive and penetrating means of bringing candidates and issues to the attention of voters. The potentialities of television will change as shifts in the interest of the television industry alter the patterns of programing within which candidates now gain access to their television audience and parties are represented.

Commercial sponsors of convention coverage and advertising agencies serving sponsors, parties, and candidates will play an obscure but influential role in the total process of nominating politics.

Candidates

For 1956 and for the future, television may widen the choice of available candidates. This may not be apparent at the moments of final choice; the main effect will probably come earlier, during the preparatory period in which the news and public affairs departments of television are bringing before the public politically available and potent personalities— and personalities are seeking to capitalize on the possibilities of television. Television may also speed the creation of political personalities.

But this capacity to create political personalities faster than any other medium gives no basis for the conclusion that a candidate who is "good television" is always going to win. The victory of Stevenson over Kefauver in 1952 illustrates that.[1] The situation might well arise in which a candidate of great reputation, won elsewhere than in front of the cameras, would so well meet the image of a desirable candidate that he could afford a good deal of loss as a camera personality and still triumph. Moreover, the way a candidate is perceived is affected by the preconceptions of the viewer; these are affected by the viewer's idea of what is appropriate to the speaker, and his previous history is as important as his current role in establishing this idea. So a man of great reputation might be able to do things with profit in front of a camera which would be harmful to another, whose public personality had been structured in somewhat different fashion.

[1] The Miami panel as a whole rated Kefauver second only to Eisenhower in making a favorable television appearance, and among the Democrats he possibly rated first. "In spite of the television impressions and the television popularity, Kefauver lost the nomination to a candidate relatively unknown to the video audience. That occurrence appears to suggest a limitation on the possible role or influence of television." Department of Marketing, Miami University, *The Influence of Television on the 1952 Elections* (1954), p. 22.

These cautions on estimating the power of television apply less forcefully when candidates combine qualities of good camera address with elements of the image of the desired candidate. Television would play a dramatic but not necessarily vital role in campaigns waged by such contestants. And all these considerations operate in a competitive context. Television may only provide the arena for charisma to battle charisma.

Current estimates of what sorts of candidates television might favor can be inferred from Republican National Chairman Leonard Hall's statement to the National Federation of Republican Women on March 1, 1955, that "we must choose able and personable candidates who can 'sell themselves' because TV has changed the course of campaigns."[2] The personable, articulate, self-possessed, but relaxed individual who can make a pleasing visit into the home of the viewer, win his attention with courtesy, and impress him with the saneness of his views and the attractiveness of his personality seems to have the current edge. It may be worth remarking that television as an instrument is neutral in the sense that if the public taste in candidates shifts, television can easily shift with it. It could bring, with equal clarity, a picture of a bombastic, ranting candidate, talking to his audiences in the home as if they were milling crowds of thousands. Television follows as much as it sets the tastes of voters in politicians. And we can be sure that all those playing a part in the presentation of candidates to the public will use the flexible resources of television to present candidates in ways conformable to beliefs about those tastes.

Evaluations to date suggest that television projects personalities better than it demonstrates issues. If this is in fact so, the reason may be that television has concentrated on personalities because of its estimate of the voter's taste. There is no reason television cannot do a great deal more

[2] *Newsweek* (Mar. 14, 1955), p. 28.

than it does to deal with issues on a reasoned basis. Competition with entertainment shows and accepted estimates of the interests and capacities of the average voter have conspired so far to counsel candidates to be brief, to be quotable, and not to put too many ideas into any one speech or program.

It is an open question whether the very existence of television will accentuate styles and swings from one to another extreme of political campaigning. The controlling factors here, it would seem, are the speed with which the political effects of a change can be sensed and the flexibility with which a move by one party can be matched by the other. Audience reports are available almost immediately, as are well-informed estimates of the impact of a move. The step-by-step treatment of the Nixon financial affair was governed by such immediate and detailed gathering of political intelligence. The question of flexibility in matching political moves presents real difficulties, if a move by one party cannot be followed without violating an essential element of the political character of the campaign waged by the other. Financial considerations may come in; the Democrats apparently wanted to match the Republican spot campaign in the closing weeks of 1952, but did not have the money to do it. (It is an open question whether the Republicans needed their spot campaign at all, or whether the Democrats lost anything by their inability to reply in kind.) But it does seem clear that if a party makes a serious campaigning innovation, the country will know about it in a moment, and if the effects are favorable and the conditions allow it, the other party can make its reply with equal promptness.

Does television inexorably and inevitably unmask the charlatan? Opinions of experts differ by 180° on this issue. One school claims it does; the other asserts that there is no better way to advance the cause of a phoney than to put him on television. Possibly a more reasonable approach would be to state that television *can* unmask a charlatan, if those responsible for use of camera and microphone want to do so. But given control over the television situation—makeup, lighting, camera angles, speechwriting, teleprompting, and the like—there is no reason in the world that the basic appearance of a candidate cannot be acceptable. (It may not be a crashing success, but there are specialists in the field of personal public relations and deportment who could get a man past either Emily Post or the casual voter.)

The selection of candidates offered to conventions and to voters will be affected by the accidents of access to the medium. Much has been made of the cost of television, and dire warnings have been sounded that the politics of the future will be the playground of the rich: candidates will be restricted to those who can afford television, or to those who are supported by the affluent. Two comments are pertinent. First, the time a major candidate buys is usually a small part of that which is available to him.[3] But second, the outlook today indicates increased relative importance for purchased time. Current interpretations by the FCC of Section 315 of the Communications Act are now being cited by the networks as reasons for further restricting the amount of time made available to any candidate on a public service basis.[4] The result would be a diminution of public discussion by candidates; discussion already limited by the understandable unwillingness of the networks to open themselves up to large public-service time demands by staging a debate between the two most prominent candidates for an office.

As purchased time gains relative importance, so the costs

[3] Often the time enjoyed as a "public figure" is granted prior to the time the person becomes a candidate within the meaning of the FCC rules and regulations; for example, that given for appearances of General Eisenhower prior to his announced candidacy.

[4] See above, pp-125, 126, 130n.

of television become more serious. These costs are set in the main within the economic context of advertising, which makes it possible for television to tap the resources of an expensive and expanding technology at the same time that costs of talent and production are driven up. The major parties will be able to obtain funds to underwrite a good deal of television, even though each will see its resources as limited and may envy the position of the other. The problem is most acute for the impecunious third party, and may tend to restrict its growth, as discussed elsewhere. Even the major parties and candidates must decide how to use funds most effectively; how to gain maximum impact without losses due to excessive repetition or to other mistakes. And their problem is eased but not settled by the circumstance that television today offers numerous opportunities for potential candidates to appear on the screen, so long as their actions and their ideas are judged newsworthy and meriting of public attention.

Candidates, potential or declared, are in general eager for access to television, but not always. As time goes on, they will become more sophisticated and skilled in using it. While few candidates will wish to incur the onus laid on the Taft faction in 1952, candidates will not always open themselves up to television. Many points and places of privacy will be defended, but in such a way as to preserve a general appearance of candor before the public. Notable in this connection is Vice President Nixon's request to the Columbia Broadcasting System not to televise his speech to the Investment Bankers Association (October 1955) on the ground that it was brief and not of major importance. He was agreeable to radio coverage, but thought that television would unduly emphasize his appearance.[5]

Television film offers parties some real advantages in pinpointing their campaigns. Conceivably this could be done

[5] *New York Times* (Oct. 12, 1955).

at the state level, where it is notoriously difficult in some areas to arrange purely state networks. But it is more important regionally in dealing with issues of regional interest and meaning, but which are not suitable or desirable for national emphasis. Such issues as public power—vital in the Pacific Northwest, but of little interest or vote-changing value in New England—can be conveniently handled by television. A single film on the subject can be economically prepared and used widely in the region, conserving the energies of the candidate for other regional or for national appearances. Television offers no solution to the candidate who would like to take one position on an issue in one region and another line on it in another. Intercommunication would be devastating. But it does give him a chance to deal efficiently with an issue on a regional basis, once he has decided how he wants to stand on the matter.

Along with increased sophistication in using television will come a revaluation of television as one among many media of communications. The novelty and gadget values have already worn off; the notion of television as a single, indispensable campaign weapon is already being revalued against the alternative possibilities offered by radio, newspapers and periodicals, and billboards. Television offers internal competition that limits its value for political communications. Television is not yet ubiquitous, either in time or space. Important political audiences cannot be reached by it today and may remain inaccessible to it. Radio reaches kitchens and automobiles; radio speaks before and during breakfast, during rides to and from work. Radio, newspapers, and billboards reach people at times and places where television does not penetrate. Most television homes are also radio homes and plenty of them are well supplied with newspapers and magazines.

Thus, the task of the planner of political communications involves a concerted and co-ordinated use of all the major media. Costs, audiences, and relative efficiency are already being weighed by such planners, and will be matched with increasing skill as time goes on.

Conventions

Television will not determine but will exercise powerful leverage on the timing, location, management, and procedure of conventions. Although plans for 1956 call for conventions in different cities, one of which is at a time extreme from the standpoint of eastern audiences, the pull of television is in the direction of placing both conventions in the same city and in a central time-space location. The cost to the networks of setting up coverage for one city is obviously less than for two, if any special preparations are required.[6] But costs aside, continuing pressure is exercised by the interest of the parties as well as the commercial sponsors in presenting the event at times when it can be seen most conveniently by the bulk of viewers. This suggests a location in the central time zone, at least until the geographical center of the population has moved further west.

Television may change some of the management problems of conventions. In the future, less space in the hall may be given to other elements of the press, partly because television has reduced their need for it.[7] Television as the relatively unobtrusive member of the visual communications family may

[6] On March 21, 1955, *Newsweek* reported that the television chains tried to get both the Republicans and the Democrats to meet in the same city, estimating an extra cost of $225,000 for each of the four networks to cover the events in Chicago and San Francisco. After the decision, some television executives talked of broadcasting only highlights of the conventions. "But," continued *Newsweek*, "they knew it was idle talk. For the competition between the chains is too sharp for any one to hold back on doing the best job it can."

[7] Needless to say, this will not happen right away. Even if a reporter plans to write his copy off a screen, he cannot tell his managing editor that, and forego a place on the floor from which to cover proceedings when they are at a climax. For the 1956 convention, press arrangements (at least for the Republicans) are in the hands of press committees themselves; possibly they can do what individual reporters cannot do in reducing total space demands to what is realistic.

be able to range more widely and penetrate more deeply than its competitors, without disturbing the decorum of proceedings or choking the aisles. The difficulty here is that a party does not want to favor one medium at the expense of others, and to open the floor to one is to open it to all. The problem is exacerbated if parties insist on keeping their delegate totals large. Preparing timetables for convention proceedings is a constant temptation to convention managers intent on making the most out of convention coverage by television. But however vocal they may be as to the extent to which they will tailor proceedings to television, experience to date suggests that the best-intentioned scheduling breaks down when the political going gets hot.

The impact of television on the procedure of the convention goes behind the formal convention itself into the related preliminaries—the work of the national committees and their subcommittees—and into the relation between the full convention and its subordinate committees.[8] The television industry is more interested in a streamlined convention procedure than it is in improved equipment or reportorial methods. Television officials would like to see the party committees conduct their preliminary meetings well ahead of the convention itself, early enough so the committee action would not telescope directly into the formal convention. And the industry would like the clearest separation in time between the work of the convention itself and the work of its subordinate committees. Such separation would spare the television newscasters, analysts, and editors the difficult choice of deciding which part of the story is the more important, and would help provide the viewer with a more comprehensive and orderly account of the convention process as a whole. When the conventions and their preliminaries overlap for the two parties, as they will in 1956, it will be difficult to achieve this orderly clarity by the simple device

[8] See above, pp. 82–91, on revised convention procedures.

of putting cameras and microphones on an event in process, with a minimum of editing and commentary. If in 1956 the Republicans were to conduct their national committee meetings several weeks in advance of the opening of the convention, they might gain sharpness of impact, avoid conflict with the Democratic convention, go to the electorate with two special events instead of one, and still fulfill the requirement of making a formal report at the convention city at the time of the convention or just prior thereto. Otherwise, the 1956 schedule will see the Democratic National Committee preliminaries in the days preceding August 13; a highly probable overlap between the final days of the Democratic convention and the Republican National Committee preliminaries; and then the Republican convention itself.

Television will tend to tighten up the proceedings of the conventions. Both the industry and the party managers would like to cut their duration and keep them moving while in session. The industry might like to see them kept to daytime hours, leaving evening prime time free for continuing commercial sales. A counterinterest is that of the networks in exploiting convention coverage as a means of demonstrating a new development or selling equipment or services. Another important counterinterest is discharging the public service responsibility of the network.

The net impact of television on convention behavior can be good. Party leaders are already aware of the fact that much convention time is devoted to long and boring operations, the product of archaic party rules. They are already taking steps to modernize them. Since the public gets its graphic view of the party at the convention, the results may inflict grave damage and weaken the ticket on election day.[9] Procedural reforms additional to those discussed above should lead to better use of delegates' time; their very in-

[9] See Arthur Krock, "To Improve Procedure at Party Conventions," *New York Times* (Oct. 8, 1954).

activity promotes the impression that the business of the party is conducted by the bosses, and that much delegate opinion is being ignored and talent wasted.

Television standards work hand-in-glove with party efforts to remedy procedural shortcomings. They call for a clean, fast-moving, interesting performance in which serious debate and detailed reporting are spiced with human interest. Interminable demonstrations or harmonica solos by sons of important local politicians make little sense on nationwide television. The goal will be short speeches, relevant and dramatic; a minimum of byplay and horseplay and sharp, clear movement toward the important decisions.

But the influence of television on these matters is often indirect and may be diffused. The pressure to put on an interesting performance does not necessarily coincide with pressure to behave reputably. Television generates both pressures, and they do not necessarily work in the same direction. What will happen depends on the response of party leaders, candidates, and delegates to their opportunities. Party leaders seem to feel, by and large, that the parties should avoid public expression of internal political conflict in the convention, as something disreputable. Hence there are frequent efforts to settle conflict privately and to make a public show of unity. At the same time, spurious unity appears both undemocratic and untrustworthy. The safe course seems to lie in allowing the appearance of a natural range of differences, for which democratic expression is permitted and which are resolved through legitimate measures: courteous and mannerly debate followed by an orderly vote under clear and acceptable rules.

Convention discipline may itself provide an undemocratic appearance, and one which shocks the general observer. Many memories today recall the instances—shown to the nation by television—in which the presiding officers of the conventions could neither see nor hear the most clamorous,

urgent, and prior demands for recognition from the floor.
Both the power of the chair and the effects of carefully arranged strategy were often obvious. Delegation chairmen
belligerently polling their delegations sometimes offered
painful contrasts to the conditions of free and judicious
choice. It goes without saying that convention indiscipline—
indifference and confusion on the floor—is equally harmful.
Television, by carrying such evidence to the nation, provides
a sanction working against such behavior.

Will television reduce or eliminate convention-hall audiences? So long as conventions are interesting and important political events, many will be interested in being there.
And the parties themselves have an interest in massive
audience participation in the event. Conventions are not
only business meetings; they are party rallies. As such they
gain special interest and fervor, and hence motivational
power, when audience participation is keen. The opportunities for vicarious identification are enhanced, and the
estimate of the value of political moves is affected by the immediate audience response. The cost of such activities—
whether spontaneous or directed—will be to the vaunted
quietness and objectivity with which television brings
politics into the living room. Nevertheless the value of
audience participation to party managers, as part of the event
and as aids to shaping the symbolic impact on viewers, will
call forth continuing efforts to assure them. But how will
party managers solve the dilemma of delegates vs. audience,
if they try to pack 4,000 delegates into a hall? Will the cast-
ing of the alternates and many delegates in the role of
audience provide a satisfactory compromise?

Campaigning

Television offers great opportunities to the parties to
wage short, incisive campaigns. Widespread, simultaneous,

geographical coverage can be achieved by films as well as by regional or national hookups, and a candidate therefore need travel less to make the requisite number of appearances. But television in itself does not reduce the number of symbolic settings in and occasions on which a candidate must appear if he is to appeal to all politically significant elements of the electorate—at least until television or a combination of political media reduces the importance of regionalism in American politics to negligible levels. The studio appearance or the fireside chat is not always an adequate formula. Speeches on farms to farmers, in plants to workers, in the North to northerners, and so forth, still require the candidate to do a bit of traveling. And he and his managers must decide how best to arrange these appearances so as to achieve optimum total effect. Choice of locale may induce resentment among persons and places not chosen, as well as provide a vicarious sense of identification and of participation. The possibility that one candidate may score relative gains by taking on a heavy schedule of personal appearances, and thus demonstrate to the electorate that he wishes to transcend the impersonalities of a merely electronic medium, poses a real threat to a campaigner who would like to operate out of a studio or from his front porch. The argument that the strength of a candidate is saved may be of no importance to one who wants to demonstrate superhuman endurance combined with respect for a wide array of groups and regions.

If, in the future, campaigns are shortened and the convention and the campaign approach a continuous flow, there will be pressure on candidates, delegates, and convention managers to turn the convention into the opening gun in a campaign that will proceed without lapse until election day. Against this pressure works a counterpressure whenever the identity of the candidate is not known in advance, and therefore there is uncertainty concerning the particular strategies and appeals which are open to the party during the campaign. It takes time to firm up strategies, complete campaign blueprints, and decide on issues and appeals to be stressed. The very act of moving without delay or hitch from choice of candidate to full-blown campaign may raise suspicion among voters that the choice of the convention was rigged or that vital political issues were being overlooked, slighted, or deliberately ignored. A political party that has just come out of a sharp factional battle (as was the case with the Republicans in 1952) usually requires time to heal rifts and make the necessary adjustments for a vigorous and integrated campaign.[10]

On balance, the most important effect of television may be on campaigning itself. Everyone seems now to agree that television has already changed campaigning; that the possibilities of multiple appearances and concentrated attention for the politically most crucial issues have reduced the time period required for a candidate to make himself and his positions favorably known to the electorate. This sort of campaign requires reduction of the issues to the strategic minimum. Selection of the issues is now a function not only of the political sagacity and information of the candidate or his managers, but also of intensive market research—a field of endeavor closely related to television as it relates to advertising and promotion. The tasks and opportunities for campaigning on television will vary with the specific issues and candidates. The chief value of television appears when one or the other candidate is relatively unknown.

Television Techniques and Interests

How will developments in television techniques and interests affect the nominating process in the future? Two

[10] There is some possible value for parties in such a condition in the example of modern post-operative surgical practice, where the patient is forced to get up and return to normal functioning without the luxury of a long bed rest.

main areas of development are of interest: (1) development of tactics and techniques by candidates and their managers, and (2) the basic plans of television for reporting political events.

Developments in the tactics and techniques of television appearances by candidates and their managers are certain; but there has not yet grown up an extensive body of professional literature on the subject, and the applicable principles, like Topsy, have "just growed." Vice President Nixon, an acknowledged good performer, summarized his tactical television credo in a speech to the Radio and Television Executives Society of New York on September 14, 1955. Refreshingly frank, the Vice President built his analysis on the assertion that "there isn't any such thing as a nonpolitical speech by a politician." And there should be no pussyfooting about television appearances. "Candidates should be prepared to spend as much money on building up a program, through advertisements and organization work, as they do on air time." Format is important; available types include political rallies, question-and-answer forums, and the intimate fireside technique. Rallies are not effective, "except as a show intended to arouse the organization members." Most useful is the intimate approach with plenty of audience participation.

It was in his comments on common television problems that Nixon was most revealing. The candidate should not read his material. He should stick to a subject he knows. "Never use television to bring up something new." Gaining the objective, the illusion of intimacy so desirable to win viewers, entails many hours of preparation. And he left the impression that, according to the *New York Times*, "there was very little done or said that could be termed genuinely impromptu."[11]

[11] "Nixon Tells How to Win TV Friends," *New York Times* (Sept. 15, 1955), p. 22.

Audiences amassed by the most popular television shows offer powerful temptation to managers and candidates, and it is likely that fresh efforts will be made by the parties to reach them. Pre-emptions are notably expensive, approximating $50,000 per hour in the case of big shows. One way to avoid pre-emptions would be to arrange well in advance with the networks and the advertisers in question to get specified dates at the usual top-show time. Thus the advertiser would protect his access to a desirable time segment; he could save the very sizable time and talent costs of several shows while getting at least an announcement that the show normally seen at this time will be seen next week, etc., or better, a courtesy line—*i.e.*, national mention—at his usual time. And the party would get at least a first chance at the audience that tunes in by habit. It would be up to the party to keep the viewer from exercising his sovereign right to switch channels or to turn off his set. But it is not always possible for a party to foresee its campaign requirements far enough in advance to make sure that it has the television time on a national network at just the moment it requires to overcome a political crisis or to cash in on a political opportunity. Some pre-emptions will undoubtedly occur.

If pre-emptions are too expensive, adjacencies remain. A favorite device of spot-advertisers is to tuck their appeals into or next to the most popular shows. Whether politicians will go in for spot campaigns in the future to the extent the Republicans did in 1952 is problematical. There is no genuine evidence that the 1952 spot campaign was necessary or effective. But in the absence of such evidence, decisions may be ruled by the concentrated interest in spots shown by many advertisers, and by the prudent counsel to clinch a victory already thought won, or to win it in the closing weeks as the Democrats did in 1948 (without benefit of spot).

Even if spots of one minute or less are not extensively

used, it now seems clear that the trend is away from the half-hour show characterized by an intimate television speech. Shorter, more incisive presentations are sought: five to fifteen-minute programs that hammer on one or two of the main themes of a party's propaganda. Such shows have the advantage of being more flexible, more easily fitted into the increasingly tight program schedules of television. They can maintain viewer interest and offer more variety than a succession of speeches in flag-draped offices. They can concentrate on the most specific and telling aspects of the major issues: farm policy; corruption in office; foreign policy; labor policy; or whatever the parties may turn up.

There will be increased exploitation of the visual capacities of television, stressing the "documentary approach." Shots of the speaker will be less frequent during his talk; his points will be illustrated. The speaker's voice, charging corruption, will be accompanied by shots of striped pants along with sleazy ones descending into a vice den; assertions of probity will be accompanied by shots of candidates and officials redolent of integrity and uprightness. Farm poverty will be shown by old dust-bowl clips; farm wealth demonstrated by shots of solid farmers alighting from Cadillacs and mounting combines.

Search for the mass audience has been combined with political appeal by the device of arraying Hollywood stars on behalf of a candidate. It now appears that political managers do not expect endorsements by such popular figures will sway many votes; as public suspicion of the value of the paid commercial has mounted, so has the political persuasiveness of the Hollywood endorsement been devalued. But people still tune in to watch stars, and such audience-bait may be of special use in attracting the non-voter to a political program.

The problem of attracting and positioning the non-voter is one in which managers of both parties have a continuing interest. The possibility that a previously inert group may enter an election and alter the balance of power is one that always threatens as well as tempts a political organization. The field is being constantly agitated by groups interested in improving citizen performance; the get-out-the-vote programs of the Advertising Council offer an example. Since this campaign characteristically exploits mass media, it is not only logical but almost imperative that the parties should try to use the same channels to draw new or inactive voters toward their candidates and causes.

The basic plan of the reporting of television may undergo serious change. To date, the industry has covered the conventions live and complete, adding to reporting of the main proceedings and decisions a filigree of commentary and human-interest angles.

Will the industry always cover the conventions complete and live? Probably not. The economic interests of television, as judged from the current pattern of sources of support, push it toward coverage that is summarized and edited. The networks have an interest in developing a form of coverage that is at once adequate from a public service point of view and that can be fully underwritten by commercial sponsors. Any changes in the economic underpinnings of the industry now in prospect will work more in the direction of more efficient coverage than to reinforce the existing pattern. If for any reason the great national advertisers reduce their television outlays for network services and programs, the networks may well have less money, either of their own or from commercial sponsors, to give the conventions exhaustive attention.

Immediate revenue from sponsors is not the only interest, however. The networks have both their public service responsibilities to consider and the competitive position of the medium to buttress, looking to sustained long-run revenues.

On balance, the television industry has less apparent incentive to give gavel-to-gavel coverage in 1956 than in earlier years. And experience in 1956 may prove crucial in precipitating a new pattern for 1960 and beyond.

It does not now look as if important new technical developments will need demonstration at conventions in future years as the medium as a whole did in 1952. Nothing other than color is in prospect for 1956, and it does not now look as if this development will be ready then.

One continuing factor making for full coverage lies in the internal competitive cross-currents of television. No network could afford to ignore the conventions to the point where no special coverage beyond news treatment would be given. If one network, not so heavily booked for time as the others, is able to cover the whole event live, it threatens the other networks with the constant danger of lost audiences or a vital news scoop.

Another factor that still works toward full coverage is the relative inexperience of television in the problems of tight editing of a complex moving story, working under conditions of considerable unpredictability of the course of events. It is easier and safer to cover everything and to transmit the picture that seems to be most interesting and important at the moment. But the effect of this factor will diminish as the editorial skill of television grows to the point where it feels more at home in dealing with the reportorial and political niceties of concentrated political reporting. Technical devices are already available, and more efficient ones are in prospect, that permit the vital points of the convention developments of an ordinary afternoon to be presented in a quarter to a half an hour, with some attention to meaningful detail. The results of votes can be quickly stated; high points of the most interesting or important speeches can be reproduced, and the story brought up to date. One mid-point in the development of such reporting would be a combination of summary and live treatment, in which film and tape summaries could be used to introduce the evening session.

Probable viewer interest in the conventions in 1956 and beyond remains an imponderable. Conceivably, conventions could become as dull as the electoral college; or, with changes in the position, role, and procedures of political parties, they could become more compelling spectacles than they are today.

It is agreed that the 1952 demonstration was a revelation to large numbers of people; even if important gains in genuine factual knowledge and insight were not registered, many voters got more of an exposure to national politics in action than they had ever had before. And they came out of the experience with a heightened sense of acquaintance and participation, and with a more immediate basis for judgment than previously had been available. In 1956, many voters will have seen a good deal of politicking both in the 1952 and the 1954 elections. Although some new voters will come, by reason of age or geography, to a new interest in the conventions, it seems likely that there will be no great new pressure for a detailed treatment. Particularly if the networks are able to deal with the 1956 conventions in a reasonably adequate and balanced manner, there need be little popular sense of political hunger if the whole event is not reported. However, if viewer interest is high, the networks will do much to satisfy it. Market research may point the way to an answer; reduced interest in 1956 will certainly alter the calculations of networks and sponsors as well as of parties.

Role of the Commercial Sponsors

Commercial sponsors of television shows, whether or not the productions are political conventions or contrived spectaculars, are interested in enormous audiences strategically situated to buy the sponsor's product; as means to that audience, they want a lively and compelling show. And in his role as good citizen of the great American community, each sponsor is interested in prominent association with public service. Most sponsors, however interested they may be personally in the outcome of an election, must also think in terms of the interests of their business. These usually require a nonpartisan stand. Only if politics were to cast up issues that involved the life or death of a business or industry would the sponsors have a large economic interest in taking a partisan position. Hence their situation is such that they can do little to influence the terms and manner in which the convention itself is managed. The main problem for them and for their advertising agencies is to arrange for an appropriate combination of sales effort and reportage. Many will continue to deplore the proximity of hucksters and huckstering to important political events. But their role in the process provides some consolations. Sponsors, by contributing to the cost of coverage, can do much to assure full and adequate coverage by radio and television.

The discussion has usually turned on a continuation of sponsorship by business or by industry. Fresh problems arise if the sponsor were to be, say, a labor union. Experience casts little light on such questions as the interest of a union in sponsoring convention coverage. Would it be in the interest of enhancing a reputation for public service? Do the unions have an interest parallel to that of a business in sales that would tend toward political neutrality? (Such an interest might arise, now that the AFL-CIO fusion has come about, for reasons of internal labor politics.) Labor unions have played substantial roles in campaigning, and have made sizable contributions to candidates or parties even if the political preference of the rank and file may have been di-

vided or in favor of the opponent. Would political parties—
one or another of the major parties, or a third party not
purely a labor party—welcome or oppose such sponsorship?
Their position, and that of the networks, is not illuminated
by the 1952 television code or the discussions leading up to
it.

Role of the Advertising Agencies

The advertising agencies play a vital and little-explored
role in the interrelationships between politics and television.
The particular role of a particular agency is governed by its
relationship to the client and by its perception of the client's
interest and how it can be advanced. Sponsors employ advertising agencies that are interested in seeing that conventions
are utilized to the hilt in the interest of the sponsor. The
resulting action extends well beyond the point of devising
the most catchy commercials, or determining how far an
advertiser can go—in good taste, or without ruining his
market—toward the "hard sell" and the viewers' bounds of
patience. Advertising agencies working for the commercial
sponsor, for a candidate, or for a political party are interested
in seeing that the convention moves along at least fast
enough to maintain audience interest. But the agency of the
sponsor also wants enough lulls to permit convenient interpo-
lation of sales messages. The agency wants its client associated favorably with the convention, and with proper frequency; the agencies working for the other interests are
equally concerned with the elements of prominence and
favorable identification for their clients. And a never-absent,
although not always overriding, interest of all these agencies
is cash. Under current practices, the networks allow the
standard commission for timebuying to the agencies for
parties and candidates—15 per cent of a sizable time fee. But
that is not their only interest. Like newspaper publishers and

other publicists, advertising men have political preferences of their own and are anxious to put their special skills at the disposal of the party or candidate of their choice. They serve with loyalty and enthusiasm.

The role of advertising agencies in devising campaign themes and strategy is hard to estimate. Many sources of ideas and strategy surround each candidate; the particular contribution of any institution cannot be generalized. But the contribution of the agencies is present, and of considerable practical and potential effect on the conduct of politics.[12] Advertising agencies are accustomed to use market research, as a means of concentrating argument, effort, and cash on those topics and in those places where a maximum of relevant effect may be expected. Such determinations, when applied to politics, tend to restrict the range of issues discussed to those that are already uppermost in the minds of those groups that are strategically placed to swing an election. (Depth interviewing might turn up some critical latent issues, however.) And the forms of statement tend to be shaped by the beliefs about communications and strategies common to commercial marketing.

The role of the advertising agency serving a political party in the pre-convention period is more generalized, if it exists at all. (The Republicans in the past have postponed selection of an agency to work with the party until after the convention. The Democrats have made their selection in advance.) The role of the party committees and officers during this period is to help the party and serve all candidates by making available technical advice on how best to use mass media or other media, and by furnishing campaign materials of a generalized character.

It is in their role as advisers and aides to candidates in the pre-convention period that advertising agencies chiefly

[12] See Stanley Kelley, *Professional Public Relations and Political Power* (in press).

affect the nominating process. Both in this period and later, the emphasis on brevity, repetition, and half-statement so common to business advertising is carried over almost automatically into the political arena.[13] When dealing with contemporary politics, advertising agencies tend to stress personal qualities rather than issues. There is also the temptation to stage events, and to make bowdlerized versions of governmental institutions and processes available through mass media, which gives pause to those interested in a serious presentation of genuine political events and institutional operations.

Madison Avenue has put noteworthy talents at the disposal of both parties during the age of radio and television; and there seems to be no reason to suppose that one side or the other can take special advantage of advertising methods for political purposes. (A party's outlays for commercial communications services are not increased if it employs an advertising agency. The agency gets its remuneration from the broadcaster or other purveyor of time, space, and services.) There is also evidence of a growing awareness among the practitioners of advertising of the values inherent in full-

[13] It should be noticed, however, that all the drives and practices of modern advertising do not move toward brevity and half-statement; some types of copy are deliberately designed to discuss issues reasonably, at length, and in such manner that they cannot be read hastily. The advertisements putting the case of the A&P to the people while civil antitrust action was pending is an example. This series of eleven full-page advertisements run in the daily press during 1949 and 1950 was the product of Carl Byoir Associates. Consider also the two full pages taken in the *New York Times* on Sept. 16, 1955 (pp. 48, 24) by Schwab & Beatty, Inc., specialists in mail-order advertising. This was an extended discussion of length of copy in advertising. Pointing out that mail-order advertising must devote considerable words to its task, the advertisement (running some 7,000 words) noted a pronounced trend toward longer copy—long enough to include every important sales message.

But compare the results of a survey of customer reaction to TV commercials reported by the American Broadcasting Company on Nov. 7, 1955. The panel preferred short commercials to comedy, "sincerity" and cartoon commercials. Most notably, they disliked commercials "in which false statements are made, high-pressure tactics are used, and presentation is too long, repetitious and exceptionally loud." This finding was said to explode the theory that the TV viewer is a 12-year-old nincompoop. *New York Times* (Nov. 8, 1955).

scale and realistic presentation of institutions and issues. Madison Avenue, when trying to shape political influence and decisions, will not always automatically apply commercial or institutional methods. The street will develop techniques responsive to the idiosyncrasies of politics as well as those of selling goods and services.

1956—A Turning Point?

However one might estimate the future of television and presidential nominating politics with the data and viewpoint of late 1955, it is certain that experience in the 1956 conventions and campaigns will do a great deal to shape the future. Evaluation of that experience by candidates, parties, networks, local stations, sponsors, advertising agencies—not to mention the audiences who are present or potential voters —may change markedly. Candidates and parties will gain fresh experience—if not laurels and wounds—on how to make the most of the convention event. They will know better what parts of a convention procedure are amenable to manipulation in the interest of the most telling television presentation. Republican scheduling of convention affairs must run the test of whether delegates will behave and whether factions will war at the wrong time as much as they harmonize for national inspection. The Democrats face unexampled problems of manipulating an enormous convention, rich in delegates and alternates, if not in spectators. There will be experience with attempts to avoid "dull Tuesday" by the smooth injection of previously hammered out convention committee reports. There will be more data on whether invocations, keynote and nominating speeches, and the activities of favorite sons can be kept within the short limits prescribed by television taste. Party in parliamentary session will vie with party rallying of supporters as central purposes of both conventions.[14]

There will also be fresh and telling data on some current imponderables that may change things markedly. What audiences can the conventions win, against possible competition from local television—better than in 1952—which is giving lookers a choice? What will the disappearance of the novelty of television do to audience size? One likely possibility is that television will not gain the proportional audience in 1956 that it enjoyed in 1952, despite the near-doubling of the number of receivers in homes. If this is the case, what will it do to the calculations of advertisers, their agencies, and the networks? Will the audience and sales results again justify a multi-million dollar outlay for full live convention coverage (plus campaign and election-night coverage)? Will the sense of public service obligation and inter-industry competition again persuade the networks that they must clear sixty to eighty hours of increasingly valuable

[14] On January 20, 1956, the Republican party used television for the first time in a nation-wide party rally, its "Salute to Eisenhower." Thirty-minutes of closed-circuit television reached 63 large party gatherings in 52 cities. The tightly disciplined show consisted of 25 shots of the meetings in eleven of the cities: Washington, New York, Chicago, Los Angeles, Boston, Cleveland, Detroit, Atlanta, Houston, Des Moines, and Portland, Oregon. Some 70,000 of the Republican party elite filled halls and auditoriums, partly to see the President or to be themselves telecast in this first national showing of the party to itself at an occasion other than the national convention. Most had paid $100 per ticket, partly to raise funds for television expenses in the forthcoming campaign.

The main political fare was the President's speech, notable chiefly for his idealistic concept of the Republican party, and his promise vigorously to support a continuation of the foreign and domestic policies of the last three years whether he runs himself or not.

The occasion raised widespread interest outside the party meetings. Television stations deluged the New York control room with requests to carry part or all of the proceedings. They were told that kinescopes would be made, parts of which could be shown after the event. Radio stations were allowed to transmit the sound signal coming from their localities. The network of the American Broadcasting Company and at least one other local Washington, D. C. station carried the President's address live. CBS and NBC, informed in advance that the President would not disclose his intentions about running, did not carry it live. Some of their outlets and many other stations repeated the address later from tape recordings.

Immediate estimates of political effects were sketchy. Some observers rated the

time for such a pair of events? What will the independent and other local stations do? How will the voters respond to the amalgam?

Thus 1956 will provide a crucial testing-time in the laboratory of political communications.

As a channel of political communication, television has not yet won to dominance, let alone monopoly. Television can multiply appearances, but only in those areas in which television reaches, at those times when television is being watched. The reach of television does not yet cover all the country, although a combination of primary and secondary impact covers almost all of the politically significant populace. Reach is not enough, however. The voter may not be looking. And television offers internal choices. Politics must compete with other fare except at those times when all networks and stations are concentrating on a political event. (And politics might conceivably compete with itself, although political managers have not yet gone in for such

---

event a stirring one. Others, in New York and Washington, noticed the similarity of behavior to that of a national convention while relatively unimportant business is going on: much talking, moving about, and inattention to the supposed center of attention, except when the President was actually speaking. These observers were also impressed by the prominent role played by the Vice President, telecast from Chicago. No other major party figure of Presidential availability, other than the President, appeared on the screen; they were speaking from cities not included in the television pickup. The rest of the speeches, other than those of Eisenhower and Nixon, were given by "little people"—a railroad engineer, a golfer, a small business man, a party functionary (who did not speak as such) and the like. Each had his set role in dramatizing one aspect of the Republican party position, reminiscent of the election-eve "Report to Eisenhower" in 1952.

In dollars and cents, the party netted $5 million. The closed-circuit hookup cost an estimated $250,000, and the party spent an undisclosed amount for halls, entertainment, box suppers, and other amenities. The consequences for party organization and finance, including the division of power between the national, congressional, state and local headquarters, are intriguing to speculate about. It seems certain that the influence of the national party headquarters will be sharply enhanced. The whole affair was a remarkable demonstration of what can be done to strengthen national party organization when a political party holds the White House under a strong and popular leader.

For accounts of the party rally, see the *New York Times*, January 21 and 22, 1956, and the *Washington Post and Times-Herald*, January 24, 1956.

direct competition.) The conventions have come closest to a monopoly of attention; campaigning has never approximated the saturation of the convention.

Even the most significant political declarations on television gain only partial audiences. No planner of political communications can yet afford to rely solely on this medium, hoping that other media will automatically take up the inevitable communications slack. Television is taking a place alongside other media—radio, newspapers, magazines, billboards, direct mail, conversation, and political rallies—that affect politics too. Mutual reinforcement among media will be sought by politicians more eagerly than communication through any single and sovereign voice.

Few new techniques in campaigning are now in evidence that take special advantage of the characteristics of television. In 1952, the major television weapon was the speech. In 1956, speeches will be reserved for the most important declarations of policy and for appearances in the most important places. But the repetitions and reinforcements will be sought by television on film, and by a host of other media uses, to be driven home in face-to-face discussion by party workers from precincts on up. The problem of the cost of television tends toward some such solution in which the necessary repetition to penetrate the voter's mind will not be made at the expense of the freshness of television or its other special qualities—or at the cost of much cash.

CHAPTER VII

Conclusions and Recommendations

I<small>N</small> <small>CONCLUSION</small>, it is in order to summarize the foregoing views and recommendations as to what should be done about the issues of public policy raised by the impact of television on the presidential nominating process.

The question of access of television to various aspects of that process proved complicated. But it seems clear that as a general principle, it can be recommended that the national committees of the parties should hold their adversary hearings in public, and probably their final sessions of full committee debate and voting as well, with freedom to go into executive session from time to time—particularly on matters that will not go to the convention in any case. A similar principle for governing access of the press to proceedings of the convention itself, and to its component committees, would seem to be in order.

The question whether television should be excluded from any sessions to which other forms of the press are given access is a different issue. Television should clearly be allowed equal access, unless it can be shown that reportage via this medium tends to distort the proceedings themselves, or their outcome, in undesirable ways. Evidence of action to date does not indicate that television is so certain to offend that it should presumptively be barred from committee or convention proceedings. The parties are already taking steps to control aspects of convention procedure that television might, in itself, tend to distort or delay.

Consideration of the question whether the television industry should be required to cover the conventions as a public service obligation led to the conclusion that no such requirement is in order. After reviewing the public service obligation of the networks under the law, the nature of the convention process at present and for the future, and the interests of the broadcasting industry in covering this as well as other important news events, it became clear that a rigid requirement was neither desirable nor necessary. Convention broadcasting is not the only form of public service that broadcasters should perform. Conventions are not always prime news, particularly when the choice is a foregone conclusion and the party is in effect going to run on its record.

Even if conventions are a vital element in our political processes, it still seems clear that full, live coverage is not necessary to an adequate discharge of the public service obligations of the networks. A combination of editing and live coverage seems to offer the most likely prospect of bringing the essence of the event to the television audience. The interest of the broadcasting industry in covering an important political event remains as sufficient guarantee that the major conventions will be given a much fuller treatment than most other special events.

Should anything be done to regulate the relations of commercial sponsors to the nominating process? Evidence and experience to date are too scattered and weak to provide a sure guide to any definite recommendations for change. The sometimes conflicting, sometimes coinciding interests of the sponsors, the industry, the parties, and the candidates have so far provided adequate defenses against any tampering by sponsors with the nominating process. And it does appear that the revenue derived from commercial sponsorship helps to provide full coverage of all aspects of the convention, and thus to bring a more detailed account to the viewer than would otherwise be provided. Whether such a detailed account is the best account, there are some doubts. A combination of live and filmed material seems, as suggested above, to give the most promise of a fully comprehensible and accurate account, in view of the inescapable conflicts in timing among various parts of the convention. Commercial sponsorship is compatible with development in this direction. The main continuing problem is to see to it that the sponsorship relationship is kept clear, and that the ever-present trap of unwarranted association of sponsor with the nominating process is avoided. Multiple sponsorship, by diffusing the number of commercial underwriters, helps accomplish this.

Review of the problem of combination of news and entertainment emphases in convention coverage disclosed no serious difficulties. Review of the techniques and procedures of news coverage suggested that more commentary, better informed and better related to the developing story of the convention as a whole, is desirable. A bare picture is not enough to keep complicated parliamentary situations clear, or to assess the factional or regional significance of committee or convention votes as they are recorded. Political sophistication among the television viewers of the nation has not yet grown to the point when these things are as clear as developments in a baseball game. The educational function of television has large scope; comment, impartial but penetrating and pungent, remains a requirement for 1956 and beyond.

The question whether the networks should state their political preferences revealed a dilemma. Public policy counsels statement of preferences when they exist, as a step required for full public understanding of what is communicated. Yet it was clear that the network services of news and news analysis have achieved a commendable standard of objectivity. And the public interest may benefit greatly from further development toward objective and impartial news services, supplemented by an effective forum in which protagonists of various points of view can illuminate all important aspects of controversial issues, including the issues involved in the choice of party nominees and candidates. Such developments might be impeded if the networks were to take partisan positions, but not necessarily so. Review of developments in the taking of an editorial position by networks suggested that there are no imminent possibilities that these editorial positions will include backing particular candidates or parties.

A final problem is the amendment of Section 315 of the Federal Communications Act, which in its present form is working to reduce access to the medium and to prevent the fullest confrontation of political candidates and issues between the major parties. The censorship provisions of the act are not wholly satisfactory and, by imposing risk on broadcasters, tend to reduce access to the medium. Amendment of the censorship provisions is not urgent, so far as protection of the body politic is concerned. Abuses have not been general or serious; candidates have not called for revolution or frequently made libelous utterances. It does seem fair and proper, however, to amend the federal law so as to protect broadcasters from libel suits arising from utterances by political candidates that they now have no power to censor. It seems more important to preserve the freedom of speech of the candidate from any unwarranted pressure from broadcasters than it is to give the broadcasters power to control the text of a political speaker while leaving them under the laws of libel. But there is no reason of public policy why they should bear risk arising from speech over which they have, under the law, no control.

The most important change in Section 315 now to be made is to render more precise the provisions governing equal time. Section 315 should be amended to require equal treatment by broadcasters of the *major parties* in their campaigns for national offices, leaving the problem of the minor parties to the more general public service obligations of the broadcasters without a rigid equal-time requirement for all of the ten or fifteen minor parties that occasionally appear on American ballots. The amendment should specify broad standards for the definition of a major political party, to be made precise by regulations issued by the Federal Communications Commission. These standards should make it possible for any party that has a reasonable chance of electing its candidates to qualify for equal time under the act. Once the broadcasting industry is not required to provide equal time for a host of candidates or of parties during the campaign period, it would become possible for them to stage debates between the candidates, or to arrange political programs that will give more adequate scope than before to the statement and confrontation of issues.

Another salutary step would be to restrict further the application of equal-time provisions in campaigns for the presidential or vice presidential nominations, to the *leading candidates* of major parties. This would be more cumbersome in administration, but would help solve the problem of political broadcasting in pre-convention and pre-primary periods. Current experience suggests that restricting equal-time provisions to those candidates of major parties (defined above) who can adduce substantial evidence of ability to poll at least 15 per cent of the vote on the first ballot in a party convention or primary, would in effect restrict application of those provisions to the leading candidates. And by so limiting the present rigid requirement for equality, the provision might well make it easier for the candidates of minor parties, or the non-leading candidates, to gain a reasonable amount of access to the medium.

In conclusion, it is well to recall the youth of television. For less than a decade has it played an active political role, and for only some four years has it played a powerful role in national politics. Scientifically speaking, very little is known about the true measure of its impact on politics or on political nominations and elections. Laymen and practitioners, both of politics and of communications arts, are rapidly developing a body of precepts and principles to guide their practices. It seems certain that television offers an unexampled resource for political communications and for the political education of the nation as one community. Television has taken its place in the spectrum of communications media. As it comes to maturity, it affords the most hope yet offered by any medium of communication for the creation of a genuinely national politics, quickly responsive to the political currents of the age.

INDEX

Index

Date Due

MAY 28 '62			